- JOURNEY THROUGH -
GOD'S WORD

ERIC SHABAN

JOURNEY THROUGH GOD'S WORD
Copyright © 2021 by Eric Shaban

All rights reserved. Neither this publication nor any part of this publication may be reproduced or transmitted in any form or by any means, electronic or mechanical, including photocopying, recording or any information storage and retrieval system, without permission in writing from the author.

Scriptures taken from the Holy Bible, New International Version®, NIV®. Copyright © 1973, 1978, 1984, 2011 by Biblica, Inc.™ Used by permission of Zondervan. All rights reserved worldwide. www.zondervan.com The "NIV" and "New International Version" are trademarks registered in the United States Patent and Trademark Office by Biblica, Inc.® Scripture quotations marked (AMPC) taken from the Amplified® Bible (AMPC), Copyright © 1954, 1958, 1962, 1964, 1965, 1987 by The Lockman Foundation. Used by permission. www.lockman.org. Scripture quotations marked (MSG) are taken from THE MESSAGE, copyright © 1993, 2002, 2018 by Eugene H. Peterson. Used by permission of NavPress. All rights reserved. Represented by Tyndale House Publishers, a Division of Tyndale House Ministries. The Holy Bible, English Standard Version (ESV) is adapted from the Revised Standard Version of the Bible, copyright Division of Christian Education of the National Council of the Churches of Christ in the U.S.A. All rights reserved. Scriptures marked (KJV) are taken from the Holy Bible, King James Version, which is in the public domain. Scripture quotations marked (WMS) are taken from The New Testament: A Translation in the Language of the People (Charles B. Williams), Copyright © 1937 by Bruce Humphries, Inc. Copyright renewed 1965 by Edith S. Williams. Used by permission. Scripture quotations marked (NLT) are taken from the Holy Bible, New Living Translation, copyright ©1996, 2004, 2015 by Tyndale House Foundation. Used by permission of Tyndale House Publishers, Carol Stream, Illinois 60188. All rights reserved.

Print ISBN: 978-1-4866-2102-6
eBook ISBN: 978-1-4866-2103-3

Word Alive Press
119 De Baets Street, Winnipeg, MB R2J 3R9
www.wordalivepress.ca

Cataloguing in Publication may be obtained through Library and Archives Canada

I dedicate this book to my Lord and Saviour Jesus Christ without whom I would have nothing to write about.

Contents

Acknowledgements — vii

Part I: The Journey of Studying God's Word

1. How My Journey Began — 1
2. How to Study God's Word — 7
3. Two Directions — 14
4. The Romans Road — 22
5. John 3:16 — 41
6. Psalm 15 — 52
7. The Full Armour of God — 65

Part II: The Journey of Applying God's Word

8. Practice What You Preach — 95
9. Enduring Trials — 114
10. The Bible and Business — 136
11. Rocky III and the Bible — 156

Conclusion — 199

Endnotes — 203

Acknowledgements

Over the past few years, I have had a strong urge to write a book, something I had never done before. Originally, I intended to take the one thousand pages of notes made throughout my many years of personal Bible study, type them out, and have them bound in a book to give to my children and grandchildren. As I began this process, it became apparent that this was not going to be something they would read—at best, they might use it for a reference.

Faced with this conundrum, I was driven by the desire to somehow take the Bible and bring it to life, introducing Bible characters who would reveal powerful truths and reveals ways in which my children and grandchildren could apply these truths to their lives. While on vacation this past year, I outlined the book with topics I thought would not only hold their interest but also show them how truly alive this incredible book could be in their daily living.

My first acknowledgement is to my wife Gail. Not only is she the love of my life, but she is also a great encouragement to me and our entire family. With Gail, I will always get the truth, and that is one of many great character traits she possesses. After writing the first seventeen pages of this book, I asked Gail what her opinion was and to let me know if it made any sense—my wife is very well-read, and I knew she would have an eye for this. After reading these pages, she told me she really liked it and encouraged me to continue. You will never know the confidence boost that gave me, and it was at this point that I began to think the book might actually happen! Gail has been with me every step of the way and was even the first person to read the completed manuscript prior to sending it to a publisher.

After completing three chapters, it became apparent that I would require someone to edit this project. Even if it was originally intended for my family's eyes only, I wanted it to read well. One day, my daughter-in-law Melanie asked me how my book was coming along, and I told her that I needed to find an editor. Melanie happened to know an editor of a Christian magazine and called him to see if he would be interested in editing my book. That is when I met Conor Sweetman, who not only completed the initial edit of my book but gave me great advice and encouragement throughout the entire editing process. I will forever be in his debt for his contribution to the finished manuscript.

The next thing I required was a publisher. My golfing buddy Mike Ajram suggested I contact Word Alive Press, which I called that afternoon and had a phone conversation with Jen Jandavs-Hedlin, who took on the publishing part of this project, for which I am grateful. It was here I was introduced to Evan Braun, who would complete the final edit of the manuscript. He pointed out some very specific things to work on and I am thankful to add his professional touch to this project. I greatly appreciate the assistance and patience shown to me by Ariana Forsman, who managed this project from start to finish.

For many years, I worked with a great marketing manager named Joe Devlin. When the book was completed, I somehow wanted Joe involved and asked him to design the front and back cover. He said he would love to; however, he knew someone who was an expert in this area. Fully trusting Joe's judgement, I was contacted by Shawn James, who did a great job in developing a front and back cover.

This book would not have happened without some very talented and godly people who contributed greatly with their study Bibles and commentaries. Whenever I study God's Word—after cross-checking all the reference verses—I turn to commentaries. A special few of these commentaries stand out without question throughout my years of study. *The MacArthur Study Bible* is always my first frame of reference. It contains twenty-five thousand explanatory notes from John MacArthur along with eighty thousand cross-references. I have listened to John MacArthur for more than thirty-five years, read a number of his books, and listened to his CDs, radio programs, and even his cassettes (I know I'm dating myself).

His study Bible is a must-have for anyone who's serious about studying the Word of God.

The next must-have resource for Bible study is a commentary. I spent a lot of time in research and concluded that by far the best one-volume commentary is *The Believer's Bible Commentary* by William MacDonald. I would also recommend the six-volume edition of Warren Wiersbe's commentary set *The Bible Exposition Commentary*.

Last and certainly not least is Chuck Swindoll, who over the past thirty-plus years has contributed through his radio ministry Insight For Living, as well as his many books and CDs. His storytelling capabilities are second to none and his love for the grace of God is paramount. *The Swindoll Bible* has been a tremendous asset.

Between those four resources, I have gained a clear understanding of any verse in the Bible that I have studied.

More than anything, the greatest acknowledgement I could give is to my Lord and Saviour, Jesus Christ, without whom I would not have even read the Bible, let alone study it and eventually write a book about it. I'm not sure whose hands this book will eventually be in, but my prayer is that anyone who reads this will have a hunger and thirst for the Word of God that can only come after entering into a personal relationship with Jesus Christ. If you're already a Christian, my hope is that this book will encourage you to spend time in the study and application of the Word of God.

Part I

The Journey of Studying God's Word

- CHAPTER ONE -
HOW MY JOURNEY BEGAN

This journey began long before I was born, and it wasn't until years later that I was introduced to the first person I would like you to meet. I've never met this individual in-person and have very little knowledge of who he was, and yet he played an enormous part in my journey through the Bible.

He was neither a pastor of a church nor a full-time minister of evangelism. He was a dry goods salesman who taught Sunday school at his local church. He was born in 1823 and lived his life for seventy-seven years before going home to be with the Lord in 1901.

This man was Edward Kimball, and to many, his name will have little meaning. However, he was responsible for changing not only my life but the lives of millions. You read that correctly—millions!

We will come back to Edward Kimball later in this chapter, but for now, let me begin the journey.

Living in a middle-class home with older brothers and two parents, my life was as normal as one could imagine. We went to school every day during the term and spent holidays mostly at home, enjoying a few vacations. I was the youngest in the family and it was a great feeling to have four older brothers who were very protective of our family—a true safety net from any trouble that came my way. Add to that a fiercely protective dad, who was a boxer in the army, as well as a mom who came the closest

I've ever seen to showing the unconditional love of Jesus, and you can see why it was a great place to spend the early years of my life.

My dad worked three jobs, and in thirteen years he amassed enough resources to start his own business. We occasionally went to Sunday school, compelled by my dad who would himself stay home with Mom. I don't recall a lot from my days in Sunday school, other than the time I dropped my pencil beside a boy in my class. When I went to pick it up, I tied his shoelaces together. When he got up, he fell, and I got into trouble.

That was pretty much my life until I was twenty years old. My dad had become very successful in his business, and I had quit school to go to work because I wanted to buy a car. (Side note: stay in school.)

Our lives were going along very well without a care in the world. Truly, I felt our family was invincible. For the most part, my brothers and I weren't living bad lives according to the standards of this world. However, speaking for myself, I would live to regret many of the things that happened, even to this day.

I can still remember vividly the phone call I received from my dad when I was twenty years old. "Don't ask questions," he said. "Just come home now."

I whipped around the corner to find an ambulance in front of the house with no flashing lights on. It was just sitting there. Then the unthinkable happened: my dad told me that my brother was gone. He'd had a very bad cold and went to bed one night at the age of twenty-four and died in his sleep.

The next few weeks were a kind of nightmare that just didn't seem to go away. My dad made all the funeral arrangements, and not long after that he sold his business and retired. He was never the same again.

The one thing I will always remember is my mom during that time. Honestly, it seemed like she cried for two weeks straight. Her grief was something I had never encountered in my life and I thought she would never recover. There was nowhere to hide and nowhere to turn; the once invincible family was shattered. Could this story ever have a happy ending?

Now, back to Edward Kimball. As the story goes, Edward Kimball was a Sunday school teacher in Detroit in 1854. There was a seventeen-year-old young man in his class who showed no interest in the lessons and appeared not to listen. This troubled Edward, so he decided to reach out to this young man outside of Sunday school. He visited the young man's workplace, where he was stacking boxes of shoes on a shelf. During the meeting, he tried to lead this young man into a relationship with Jesus Christ, but he left feeling it had been unsuccessful and went home.

Well, it turned out to have been a very successful meeting indeed. The young man was Dwight L. Moody, who went on to become one of the greatest evangelists in the history of the world. He also founded the Moody Bible Institute, which is still a vibrant university to this day.

That is not where the story ends. Through the ministry of Dwight L. Moody, Frederick Brotherton (F.B.) Meyer came to faith in Jesus Christ and became a pastor in London, England. Meyer introduced Moody to other churches, ministries, and chapels in England and then joined Moody in America to minister together. The two preachers became lifelong friends.

F.B. Meyer was a great influence, bringing John Wilbur Chapman of Richmond, Indiana into a personal relationship with Jesus Christ. Chapman began preaching with Moody and travelled as a full-time evangelist, working with Moody at a world fair and hosting many meetings of his own. On one occasion, he hired someone to travel ahead of him in advance of a meeting. This man was Willian Ashley Sunday, and by this happenstance, Billy Sunday began his own evangelical ministry. Billy Sunday went on to play a major role in the conversion of Mordechai Ham, who then went on to lead thousands to Christ.

As Mordechai Ham presented the gospel one November evening in Charlotte, North Carolina in 1934, something happened. It was the final night of meetings when a tall sixteen-year-old young man walked the aisle to receive Jesus Christ as his Saviour and Lord. His name was William Franklin Graham, whom we now know as Billy. The rest, as they say, is history. Billy Graham went on to be the greatest evangelist in history, preaching to millions over his lifetime and living to be ninety-nine years old before he went home to be with the Lord.

So one lowly Sunday school teacher influenced millions, of which I am one. Who knows where this story of Edward Kimball will end? The only end I can think of is the Lord welcoming him home by saying, "Well done, good and faithful servant."

After my brother passed, my mom was in the throes of the deepest grief I had ever encountered. She seemed to give up completely, and there seemed to be no end in sight.

Out of sheer desperation, she wrote a letter to Billy Graham, pouring her heart out. Not long after, a response came—not from Billy Graham, but from his organization. Whatever they sent to my mom, she was suddenly filled with hope. It was truly quite miraculous!

Shortly after that, my mom began to attend church and she told us she had received Jesus Christ as her Lord and Saviour and dedicated her life to the service of God.

As an eyewitness, I can tell you this was more than mere words for Mom; she went straight into action. The only thing Mom wanted to talk about was Jesus. She typed an exceptionally long letter explaining the beauty of salvation and sent it to every family member and friend she had. She even sent it to a Jewish rabbi!

From that day forward until she went home to be with the Lord, I never saw my mom bent under the weight of great grief again. Even when the doctor told her she had cancer and would soon pass away, her response was, "Well, I guess the Lord is calling me home."

I took a different road, which today I am not proud of and about which I still carry regret. There were many nights when I came home to my parents' house very drunk. Consistently, I would find a letter on my bed from my mom telling me about Jesus and how much He loved me. Though I had been drinking, I would read the long letters in their entirety, knowing Mom would ask questions the next day. She prayed for me every day for years to come, that I might know Jesus as my Lord and Saviour.

My life stayed the same for the next few years, until I met the love of my life. She saw me drunk one night at twenty-four years old and told me she didn't want to have anything more to do with me. I told her that if it was a problem, I would put an end to the drinking. I'm not too sure if she really believed me, but we got married, and I've kept that promise for forty-two years.

Everything in my life changed one night while sitting in a stadium with my wife, who was then pregnant with our first child. There were thousands of people in attendance, and we were seated almost at the back of the stadium. The stage looked very small from our vantage point. The Billy Graham crusade had invaded our city and the stadium was packed every night with people eager to hear the famous evangelist.

Billy Graham began to preach on the topic of loneliness. At that point, my life felt full, as the only thing I truly wanted was to be a dad; this had to do with the love and respect I had for my dad. So here I was, with the love of life and about to become a dad!

Billy Graham went on to say that no matter what you have in life, you will eventually experience a deep loneliness, as there will always be a void in your heart that can only be filled with Jesus Christ. Never in my life had I felt so lonely, and honestly, I thought he was speaking directly to me. He then discussed the love of Jesus, who had died for my sins, and explained that I had to repent of those sins and ask Jesus into my heart in order to fill the void. He then asked people to come forward if they wanted to receive the gift of God that night—right at that moment, in front of thousands of people.

I immediately said to my wife, "I have to go." Incredibly, she grabbed my hand and came with me.

That night, I dedicated my life to Jesus Christ. Just as I finished receiving Jesus as my Saviour, standing in front of the stage, a woman tripped over a television cable on the ground and I caught her. It was my mother! She had seen us come forward as she was singing in the choir. Makeup was running down her face as she cried tears of joy. I will never forget that moment.

Over the years, our family grew to four children and four grandchildren, and I experienced great success in my career.

With this background established, I'd like to get down to the reason I wrote this book in the first place. As my walk with Jesus deepened year after year, another passion took over my life; the Bible, the Word of God, is the most amazing book I have ever read and studied. Studying God's Word changed my life and I hope to introduce you to some of the biblical characters I have met and show you how they answered every question I had in every situation.

It is my prayer that the thirty-plus years of study I have put into this book will give you opportunities to not only love the Bible but apply its precepts to your life. It is the only authoritative Word of God.

- Chapter Two -

How to Study God's Word

So, why did I begin to study the Word of God? What was my deep theological reason for taking this lifelong journey? I wish I could give you a really spiritual reason, but I don't have one.

When my wife and I started going to church, we took everything at face value—almost a blind faith. Eventually, I found myself questioning things that people said and preached; usually the reaction was not positive. I was told by others that if I had a problem with Scripture, I should take it up with God.

Needless to say, this was a frightening thought at first. But as time went on, certain things began to not make sense to me and I found myself facing a dilemma: I knew following Christ was the answer, but I realized that preachers were as mortal and fallen as I was.

Please don't misunderstand me. There are great preachers of the Bible, and I've known and befriended many. I truly believe there is no greater vocation on earth than preaching the Word of God. However, we are also responsible to test and know God's Word. 2 Timothy 2:15 commands, *"Do your best to present yourself to God as one approved, a worker who does not need to be ashamed and who correctly handles the word of truth."* In the last thirty-plus years of my life, I have studied more than one thousand Bible verses and yet I am far from being an expert, though I certainly have a good grasp on some major points in Scripture.

Something else happened on my way along this journey. I began to crave my time in God's Word, wanting to learn as much as I could.

Then I came across Matthew 5:6, which tells us, *"Blessed are those who hunger and thirst for righteousness, for they will be filled."* The more I studied, the more I realized how holy God was and how sinful I was. So I greatly encourage you to spend time in God's Word and develop the hunger and thirst that comes from His Holy Word.

I've heard of many different methods of studying the Bible, but many years ago while attending a conference at our church we streamed a leadership seminar from Willow Creek Community Church. These seminars always featured incredible leaders, not only from Christian circles but from business and other fields. The seminar was so good that I spoke about it with the managers I worked with, and they attended it with me for several years afterward.

During one of the sessions, our church decided to use a Bible study format introduced by the seminar. It was called BROAM, and it immediately hit home for me. It fit perfectly with my style of study. Since then, I've used it for all the studies I've done and I've trained many on how to use it.

In this chapter, I will take the time to explain the BROAM method and give you a few examples. There is an expression that says, "Give a person a fish, and you'll feed them for a day. Teach a person to fish, and you'll feed them for a lifetime." That's what BROAM accomplished.

Let's begin with what the word stands for:

- Background
- Read
- Observation
- Application
- Memorization

First, you need to identify the right tools for the job, and there are some specific tools required to dig into the Word of God. You need a study Bible, a commentary, and a Bible dictionary. These are essential for studying and understanding God's Word. Believe me, the investment is well worth it and will pay incredible dividends in your life.

A study Bible usually includes an explanation about the author of each book of the Bible, as well as an outline of the book's theme. Further, Jesus's words are identified with red lettering and commentaries explain the meaning of verses and provide cross-references with other coinciding verses. Reviewing these simple features will radically change your view of the Bible. *The MacArthur Study Bible* is one of the best I've seen and I would highly recommend it.

Next, you need a Bible commentary, which takes each verse of the Bible and provides a detailed explanation of it.

Lastly, a Bible dictionary will provide you with scriptural definitions.

Once you have all three resources, you're ready to unpack the Word of God and make it come alive in your life and daily living!

BACKGROUND

Start by choosing a verse or portion of Scripture that you love and want to understand deeper. The greatest aspect of this method of study is that you can basically choose any verse. Some people choose entire chapters of the Bible.

Regardless of whether you choose a verse or an entire chapter, the background requires you to first identify four key details about the passage: who, what, where, and why. Who wrote it? Find out as much as you can about the author and who the audience was. Then, what was the author trying to say? This refers to the theme of the verse or chapter. An important part of the background is where the scripture was written. As an example, the letter to the Philippians was written in the city of Philippi, which means "city of Philip," named after Philip II of Macedon (the father of Alexander the Great). Next, why did the author write it and what were the circumstances surrounding the verse or chapter? You will be amazed at how much more you'll understand about the passage after getting to know these things.

READ

This may sound simple—and it is—but there's a reason to read and re-read the passage of scripture. People often take a specific verse out of context, which is why it's important to not only read the verse alone, but also the verses that surround it. Read the passage four or five times to get a true feel for what the author is trying to say.

Now you'll move into the most important phases of your study: observation and application.

OBSERVATION

This is where your new mini-library will come into play. You'll also need your laptop or pen and paper because it's important to document your research. Again, my suggestion at first is to undertake a verse-by-verse study. If you've chosen a chapter, take your time and break it down one verse per day, or one verse per week. This is not a race! Enjoy this opportunity to mine for treasures in God's Word.

The first thing you need to do is break down the verse into segments. (I'll show you an example at the end of this chapter.) After breaking down the verse using your study Bible, review all the reference verses found in the margin of your Bible. Also read all the notes included about the verse, usually found at the bottom of the page.

Secondly, take out your Bible commentary and read the detailed explanation written by biblical scholars. You may not agree with everything that is written in it, but it will offer you alternative views.

APPLICATION

This is by far the most important step in the process. Now that you've dissected the verse and gained a clearer understanding of it, ask yourself this question: what are you going to do with this newfound information? James 2:17 says, *"In the same way, faith by itself, if it is not accompanied by action, is dead."* You have to use what you have learned.

When writing down applications, keep in mind that you want to identify things you can start to do immediately. Through this process, you will develop within yourself a new desire for the things of God. Ephesians 2:10 says, *"For we are God's handiwork, created in Christ Jesus to do good works, which God prepared in advance for us to do."* This verse is directed at Christians, and it means that God has created us to do good things.

When you choose an application from your completed study, don't be afraid to take it out for a test drive.

MEMORIZATION

The final step in the process is to memorize the verse you've been studying. Why? As Psalm 119:11 explains, *"I have hidden your word in my heart that I might not sin against you."* That, my friend, is the answer, in a nutshell. So many great verses in the Bible can be used to hold you accountable for the next step you're about to take. Armed with Scripture and the Holy Spirit, you are preparing yourself to become a servant of the Most High God.

Before we go any further, let's start with an example of the BROAM process in action. We'll use this scripture:

> *Blessed is the one who does not walk in step with the wicked or stand in the way that sinners take or sit in the company of mockers, but whose delight is in the law of the Lord, and who meditates on his law day and night.*
>
> —Psalm 1:1–2

Background. David wrote seventy-three of the one hundred fifty psalms in the Bible.[1] Most people think he wrote them all, but he only wrote about fifty percent of them. This particular psalm, which David did write, would be classified as a "wisdom psalm," as it offers guidelines for godly people.

Psalm 1 opens by dispelling the common illusion that the sinful life is the good life. We are being brainwashed every day into thinking that true and lasting satisfaction is found by indulging the lusts of the flesh and dismissing the life of purity. But here the psalmist sets the record straight. Also note that the word "blessed" in Hebrew means, "Oh, how very happy."[2]

Observation. What does this verse say? Let's break it down:

- Blessed is the one
  - who does not walk in the council of the wicked

- or stand in the way that sinners take
- or sit in the company of mockers,
- but whose delight is in the law of the Lord,
- and who meditates on his law day and night.

There are two cross-referenced verses to go along with this passage. Psalm 40:4 says, *"Blessed is the one who trusts in the Lord, who does not look to the proud, to those who turn aside to false gods."* And Psalm 128:4 says, *"Yes, this will be the blessing for the man who fears the Lord."*

Notice in the first verse how the person is spiralling downward. He begins by walking, then standing and then sitting. This is a great picture of how subtly sin can enter your life, seeming without harm at first before slowly dragging you deeper and deeper into it.

Commentator Charles Ryrie wrote, "This psalm stands as a faithful doorkeeper to the entire Psalter. It reminds those who enter of the righteous behaviour and fruitful life that are characteristic of the one who delights in God's law."[3]

Application. I see six applications that could be implemented immediately:

1. If I follow this passage, I should expect blessings.
2. I should not be in the presence of wicked people who do wrong things.
3. I should not be in the presence of people who willfully commit sinful acts.
4. I should not sit with people who make fun of others.
5. I should love to read and study God's Word and anticipate great joy from the experience.
6. My mind should be focused on God's Word all day and night.

As you can see, you can get a lot out of a few Bible verses. This covers just two verses in the midst of the entire Bible, an enormous resource to help you to live your life. Just think of what would happen if you did this on a consistent basis!

Memorization. Now we come to a vital part of the process, and that is memorizing the scripture you have just studied. As you apply it to your life, you will find that saying the verse over in your mind will bring to light all you have learned. I repeat to myself Psalm 119:11: *"I have hidden your word in my heart that I might not sin against you."*

So where do you start?

- Pick any verse of Scripture and try out this method.
- Pray that God will speak to you through His Word.
- Note the words of James 1:22, which says, *"Do not merely listen to the word, and so deceive yourselves. Do what it says."*
- Your life will change.

Please take up this challenge and study a verse today! May God truly richly bless your study of His Word.

- Chapter Three -

Two Directions

The only way to begin this journey on earth is to start at the end. Truly this is a life and death decision. You've heard it said, "Two things in life are certain: death and taxes." When death does occur, it is vital to know what's next.

After coming home from the Billy Graham crusade, I realized that things had to change. Shortly after that life-changing experience, our first child was born and my immediate thought was that I would never want my daughter to end up with someone like me. Decisions had to be made, and what better place to start than by listening and acting out the words of Jesus Himself?

The rest of this chapter will show the two opposing directions we all face in areas of our lives. In my own journey, I needed to choose whether to follow my own desires or follow Jesus.

Jesus delivered the greatest sermon ever heard when He preached the Sermon on the Mount. This chapter will focus on the end of the sermon, found in Matthew 7:13–25.

Throughout this chapter, I want to attempt to bring the Bible to life. As we journey through the various two possible directions of many areas of this section of Scripture, I want you to imagine that I am actually speaking with Jesus.

TWO FEARS

I want to start with something God said through the wisest man in history, Solomon: *"The fear of the Lord is the beginning of knowledge, but fools despise wisdom and instruction*" (Proverbs 1:7). With that in mind, think of everything you've learned in your life from the time you started to walk until now. The learning curve of life is steep, and we never stop learning. Even people with multiple degrees know this to be true; the thirst for knowledge is never-ending.

It amazes me that the wisest man who ever lived explains that the beginning of knowledge is the fear of the Lord! Yes, that is where knowledge truly begins. Matthew 6:33 says, *"But seek first his kingdom and his righteousness, and all these things will be given to you as well."* What things? Everything! No matter what comes your way, good or bad, if you seek first His kingdom, you will have a Saviour and Lord along with you on this journey. Even when Jesus began the Sermon on the Mount, he said, *"Blessed are those who hunger and thirst for righteousness, for they will be filled"* (Matthew 5:6). Knowledge begins with God, the Creator of the universe.

Today, most people have no fear at all for the Lord. Romans 3:18 says, *"There is no fear of God before their eyes."* Most don't even believe in God, let alone view Him as holy and the Creator of the universe. Even those who don't believe in God feel that He is one who loves people and would never harm anyone, let alone send anyone to hell. He is the God of love and mercy, but also the God of justice.

Therefore, the two fears of the Bible are clear: either fear God or don't fear God.

TWO GATES

As my journey began, I found myself staring at two gates—and it was here where I realized an important decision had to be made. I sensed that my life would change completely depending on which gate I walked through.

One gate was large and wide, and droves of people were going through it very easily. They seemed to have not a care in the world. However, the huge sign above the gate spelled out the word *Destruction*.

There was another gate, this one small and narrow and only a few could pass through it at a time. The line was small, and it was difficult to get through the gate. The small sign hanging above it simply said *Life*.

Today, people have a very relaxed view of hell. It's real! John MacArthur explains in his commentary:

> Jesus is drawing the line as clearly as possible between the way that leads to destruction and the way that leads to life (Matthew 7:13–14). Both the narrow and wide gates are assumed to provide the entrance to God's kingdom. Two ways are offered to people. The narrow gate is by faith, only through Jesus, constricted and precise. It represents salvation in God's way that leads to life eternal. The wide gate includes all religions of works and self righteousness, with no single way but it leads to hell not heaven.[4]

Further, Acts 4:12 tells us, *"Salvation is found in no one else, for there is no other name under heaven given to mankind by which we must be saved."*

When I met Jesus on my journey, I found that He was waiting for me to make my decision. What would I do? He explained to me that following Him was a very difficult road to take, as it was a completely different road from that which the world would follow—and yet, it would lead to everlasting life.

As for the road marked *Destruction*, it was clear that it led to everlasting torment.

Jesus then explained that everything in life needs to be viewed from the point of view of eternity, or else I would never have a clear picture of life after my time on earth was finished.

John MacArthur also wrote,

> The gate is narrow. Christ continually emphasized the difficulty of following him. Salvation is by grace alone but is not easy. It calls for knowledge of the truth, repentance, submission to Christ as Lord, and a willingness to obey his will and word.[5]

How do I know which gate to walk through? The two choices are the narrow gate and the wide gate.

TWO TEACHERS

As I looked around the area with the two gates, I noticed many teachers talking about the various ways in which a person can live their life. They presented their points of view with great eloquence and were very persuasive.

Then I heard Jesus say, "*I am the way and the truth and the life. No one comes to the Father except through me*" (John 14:6).

"Who are these teachers?" I asked Him.

He then explained that their teachings were false. Outwardly, they looked interesting and had excellent communication skills, but inside they were ferocious wolves who would tear your life apart with their teaching.

"They are from their father, the devil," Jesus said. "If you listen to them long enough, you will find that their teaching is not sound. Their actions will speak louder than their words."

I then met an apostle whom Jesus loved, and his name was John. He wrote in 1 John 4:1, "*Dear friends, do not believe every spirit, but test the spirits to see whether they are from God, because many false prophets have gone out into the world.*"

This is when it became clear that the only way to test and trust what people said was to really get to know God. To do that was to understand that the only authority is the Bible, God's Word—and at this point, things started to become clear. Right was right, even if everyone else said it was wrong, and wrong was wrong, even if everyone said it was right.

Therefore, the two teachers of the Bible are false teachers and biblical teachers.

TWO TREES

Jesus then told me, "You can learn an awful lot about a person by what they say and do. Actions speak louder than words."

He then went on to explain that a good tree bears good fruit, but a bad tree bears bad fruit. To reinforce this point, He went on to say, "*A good tree cannot bear bad fruit, and a bad tree cannot bear good fruit*" (Matthew 7:18).

From this, I understood that one would pick the fruit of a good tree either to eat or sell.

But then I asked, "What happens to the bad tree?"

"They will be thrown into the fire," Jesus answered.

"What else would one do with bad trees?"

And He said, "Thus, by their fruits you will recognize them."

And so the two trees of the Bible are the good tree and the bad tree.

TWO PEOPLE

Then Jesus reminded me of a parable from Luke 18:9–14, explaining that self-righteous people tend to look down on others.

I have found in my own life that some people, because they have some type of religious background, feel they have the implicit right to look down on others. There is no doubt that it's a privilege to know Jesus as your Lord and Saviour, but that doesn't give us the right to think ourselves better than others. If anything, the more I came to know Jesus and His holiness, the less I thought of myself.

How could the God of the universe care or even think about me? The longer my journey continued, the clearer it became how small and menial my role is compared to the plan of salvation for the world.

As Jesus and I stood in front of a temple, we saw two people come to pray. It was clear from their appearances that one person was a very religious man, dressed in robes and with a look of authority; Jesus identified him as a Pharisee.

A second man showed up, and he was an everyday guy with no appearance of authority. He looked troubled and broken. Jesus said this man was a tax collector.

These were two very different people, but both of them were coming to the temple to pray.

Jesus told me to pay attention and watch these men communicate with their Father. The Pharisee looked up and began to pray, saying, "God, I thank You that I am not like other people—robbers, evildoers, adulterers—or even like this tax collector. I fast twice a week and give a tenth of all I earn."

I couldn't believe my eyes when he pointed at the tax collector and said, "I'm not like him." This is part of what originally made me want to study God's Word, because so many people feel like this Pharisee. I could tell immediately this was not the way to pray and communicate with Almighty God.

I felt very discouraged, and Jesus told me to wait.

The tax collector couldn't even step forward, as he didn't feel worthy to even be in the temple. You could see that he was troubled right down to his soul and was in desperate need. He bowed his head, unable to even look up to heaven.

I truly felt for the man and wanted him to find what he was looking for from God.

The man began to beat his breast—what anguish he had!—and then finally spoke: "God, have mercy on me, a sinner."

Wow! What a powerful petition that was to our Creator God—simple and to the point. Nothing else was necessary.

Jesus says in Luke 18:14, *"I tell you that this man, rather than the other, went home justified before God. For all those who exalt themselves will be humbled, and those who humble themselves will be exalted."*

Recently I heard someone describe humility this way: "It's not about thinking less of yourself but thinking of yourself less."

Therefore, the two types of people in the Bible are Pharisees and tax collectors.

TWO CATEGORIES

In Matthew 7:21, Jesus says, *"Not everyone who says to me, 'Lord, Lord,' will enter the kingdom of heaven, but only the one who does the will of my Father who is in heaven."* In my estimation, this is without a doubt one of the scariest verses in all of Scripture.

Can you imagine going through your whole life and later finding out that you weren't saved by Jesus? Going back to the beginning of this chapter, we find that this is essentially a life-and-death decision. By this, I don't mean that we have to work our way into the family of God through

Jesus, but there must be real fruit in your life to show that a change has occurred. There must be a difference.

Further, Jesus says, *"Many will say to me on that day, 'Lord, Lord, did we not prophesy in your name and in your name drive out demons and in your name perform many miracles?'"* (Matthew 7:22) This group was trying to work their way into heaven, but we could never do enough to earn that. Their entire confidence was built on the signs, wonders, and works they had done.

In Matthew 7:23, Jesus concludes by saying, *"Then I will tell them plainly, 'I never knew you. Away from me, you evildoers!'"*

And so the two categories in the Bible are those who do God's will and those who don't.

TWO FOUNDATIONS

I was still reeling over what might be one of the most dreaded verses in the Bible when Jesus wanted to talk to me about building houses. He discussed with me people who listened to Him and implemented what He had said, as opposed to those who listened and did not respond.

He then mentioned the words of James: *"Do not merely listen to the word, and so deceive yourselves. Do what it says"* (James 1:22). This was not a discussion about doing good deeds to get into heaven. Rather, James was speaking to other followers of Jesus.

The first builder was a person who listened to the Word of God and put it into practice on a daily basis. Jesus said,

> *Therefore everyone who hears these words of mine and puts them into practice is like a wise man who built his house on the rock. The rain came down, the streams rose, and the winds blew and beat against that house; yet it did not fall, because it had its foundation on the rock.*
>
> —Matthew 7:24–25

It became clear to me that this was the same person who had gone through the narrow gate that led to everlasting life. Even with all the trials and tribulations that were thrown at him throughout life, he was able to stand, because his rock was Jesus and his foundation was the Word of God. Nowhere did Jesus say that life as a Christian would be easy—if anything, He said it would be very difficult. The difference-maker is that the Rock is stronger than anything on this earth.

Jesus then went on to discuss the second builder, who heard His words but did not take action:

> *But everyone who hears these words of mine and does not put them into practice is like a foolish man who built his house on sand. The rain came down, the streams rose, and the winds blew and beat against that house, and it fell with a great crash.*
> —Matthew 7:26–27

William MacDonald wrote, "The world considers a wise man to be someone who lives by sight, who lives for the present, and who lives for self; Jesus calls such a person a fool."[6]

John MacArthur elaborates,

> The house represents a religious life, the rain represents divine judgement. Only the house built on the foundation of obedience to God's Word stands, which calls for repentance, rejection of salvation by works and trust in God's grace to save through the His merciful provision.[7]

After listening to Jesus, I truly wanted the Rock to serve as the foundation of my life. The two possible foundations in the Bible are these: rock and sand.

Now it was time to put my words and thoughts into action, but there were questions that needed to be answered. Which way? How do I get eternal life? How do I make sure I can get through the narrow gate?

- Chapter Four -

The Romans Road

The next person I met on this journey through the Bible was Paul. I was stopped dead in my tracks by this man's incredible story! Let's see how Paul came to know Jesus, as recorded in Acts 9:1–19:

> But Saul, still breathing threats and murder against the disciples of the Lord, went to the high priest and asked him for letters to the synagogues at Damascus, so that if he found any belonging to the Way, men or women, he might bring them bound to Jerusalem. Now as he went on his way, he approached Damascus, and suddenly a light from heaven shone around him. And falling to the ground, he heard a voice saying to him, "Saul, Saul, why are you persecuting me?" And he said, "Who are you, Lord?" And he said, "I am Jesus, whom you are persecuting. But rise and enter the city, and you will be told what you are to do." The men who were traveling with him stood speechless, hearing the voice but seeing no one. Saul rose from the ground, and although his eyes were opened, he saw nothing. So they led him by the hand and brought him into Damascus. And for three days he was without sight, and neither ate nor drank.
>
> Now there was a disciple at Damascus named Ananias. The Lord said to him in a vision, "Ananias." And he said, "Here I am, Lord." And the Lord said to him, "Rise and go to the street called Straight, and at the house of Judas look for a man of Tarsus named Saul, for behold, he is praying, and he has seen in a vision a man named Ananias come in and lay his hands on him so that he might

regain his sight." But Ananias answered, "Lord, I have heard from many about this man, how much evil he has done to your saints at Jerusalem. And here he has authority from the chief priests to bind all who call on your name." But the Lord said to him, "Go, for he is a chosen instrument of mine to carry my name before the Gentiles and kings and the children of Israel. For I will show him how much he must suffer for the sake of my name." So Ananias departed and entered the house. And laying his hands on him he said, "Brother Saul, the Lord Jesus who appeared to you on the road by which you came has sent me so that you may regain your sight and be filled with the Holy Spirit." And immediately something like scales fell from his eyes, and he regained his sight. Then he rose and was baptized; and taking food, he was strengthened.

—Acts 9:1–19, ESV

So, who was Paul? His Hebrew name was Saul, and his Greek name was Paul. He was born in Tarsus and was of the tribe of Benjamin. He was also a Roman citizen, born around the time of the birth of Jesus. During his time as a Jewish scholar, under a celebrated rabbi named Gamaliel, Paul took part in the violent persecution of Christians. Like his father before him, he was a Pharisee of the strictest Jewish sect.

This is how Paul is described in Philippians 3:4–6:

…though I myself have reasons for such confidence.

If someone else thinks they have reasons to put confidence in the flesh, I have more: circumcised on the eighth day, of the people of Israel, of the tribe of Benjamin, a Hebrew of Hebrews; in regard to the law, a Pharisee; as for zeal, persecuting the church; as for righteousness based on the law, faultless.

In addition to this zealous pharisaic track record, I also learned that he wrote two-thirds of the New Testament. What a change God wrought in his heart!

It was Paul's words in the book of Romans that showed me how to receive eternal life through Jesus Christ our Lord. Most of the verses we will discuss in this chapter are from the book of Romans, with a few verses from Ephesians (which Paul also wrote), and the book of John.

Early on, I realized there is only one way to God. In John 14:6 our Lord Jesus said, *"I am the way and the truth and the life. No one comes to the Father except through me."*

Well, that sort of simplified things for me, but how do you do that? Paul then explained how to know for sure that you're a Christian, a follower of Jesus Christ. I can tell you that I was all ears; this would be the most important decision of my life!

Let's travel together down the Romans Road.

In Romans 3, Paul makes something very clear: *"As it is written: 'There is no one righteous, not even one'"* (Romans 3:10). Mankind is universally evil.

When you see the term "it is written," know that this usually means there's a reference in the verse to an Old Testament text. In this case, it's a reference to Psalm 14:1, which says, *"The fool says in his heart, 'There is no God.' They are corrupt, their deeds are vile; there is no one who does good."*

That certainly made it clear for me. There wasn't much room left for open debate on that topic.

While reflecting on this verse, I realized that it's important not to have such high expectations of other human beings; none of us can do anything good. So where does our righteousness come from then?

Just to make it crystal clear, Paul went even further a little later in the chapter: *"This righteousness is given through faith in Jesus Christ to all who believe. There is no difference between Jew and Gentile, for all have sinned and fall short of the glory of God…"* (Romans 3:22–23) I was therefore faced with another choice between two groups: the faithful and the faithless.

John MacArthur wrote, "God bestows his righteousness on all who believe, Jew or Gentile, because all people—without distinction—fail miserably to live up to the divine standard."[8]

The World's Bible Dictionary refers to righteousness this way: "Though righteous deeds, or good works, cannot save anyone, once people are saved their lives should be full of righteous deeds. Once God declares them righteous, they must make it true in practice by living righteously."⁹

To bring home the point, Isaiah 64:6 says, *"All of us have become like one who is unclean, and all our righteous acts are like filthy rags."*

It was becoming very clear to me that I could never earn my way into heaven and that my definition of righteousness and God's definition were two different things.

In Matthew 5:20, Jesus made it clear that righteousness was out of reach: *"For I tell you that unless your righteousness surpasses that of the Pharisees and the teachers of the law, you will certainly not enter the kingdom of heaven."*

These verses caused me to desire to know the righteousness of God and how it could become the centre of my life. The term "saved" came up again and again in my journey, and I wanted to know more about that, so I had to determine what I would be saved from.

Realizing that I would be dealing with eternal life and God, I wanted to know everything I could and realized that entering the narrow gate wasn't going to be an easy task. I was a sinner who needed to be saved. That was clear. But how?

Next, Paul explained to me that Jesus had died on the cross for my sins, and it was through Him that one could be saved. Romans 5:6–8 says,

> *You see, at just the right time, when we were still powerless, Christ died for the ungodly. Very rarely will anyone die for a righteous person, though for a good person someone might possibly dare to die. But God demonstrates his own love for us in this: While we were still sinners, Christ died for us.*

These are amazing verses of Scripture, as they show that no one would naturally fit into this category of righteousness. And yet God loved us so much that He sent Jesus to die for sinners. All have sinned, yet God was willing to die for us!

There had to be more to this story, and as I continued to read Paul's words, I found that there was certainly more to come, including expectations and conditions to following Jesus if I wanted to be saved from eternal damnation.

It was starting to get serious and Paul had my full attention. Being saved from hell was something I wanted to make sure I understood.

Today, many churches seem to make it extremely simple to become a Christian and join the family of God. He is loving, caring, and has enormous mercy and grace, and I would come to know this as true. But He is also a God of justice.

I truly want to be on the side of a loving heavenly Father, but I had to follow Paul through this process.

The next passage Paul wanted to discuss revealed not only the love of God but also the judgement of God. He plainly explains what happens spiritually when unforgiven sin exists in someone's life: *"For the wages of sin is death, but the gift of God is eternal life in Christ Jesus our Lord"* (Romans 6:23). Note that the most important word in this verse is *but*.

Paul explained to me that there is no one, not even one person, who is without sin, and when we sin we are destined to an eternity of damnation in hell. At this moment, I began to praise God in my heart for a way of escape. I had finally found what I wanted in my life.

William MacDonald states,

> The apostle summarizes the subject by presenting these vivid contrasts:
> - Two masters—sin and God
> - Two methods—wages and free gift
> - Two aftermaths—death and eternal life[10]

This is a great description of this verse, and I looked forward to receiving this free gift from God.

As I dove further into the Bible, I became more and more thankful for the hope that God gives me in Jesus Christ.

As John MacArthur explains, "This verse describes two inexorable absolutes 1) spiritual death is the paycheck for every man's slavery to sin 2) eternal life is a free gift God gives undeserving sinners who believe in his Son."[11]

Paul then took time to explain the process of receiving this free gift, the greatest gift in all the world.

My life was on the verge of changing in a way I had never thought possible. Forgiveness of sin, eternal life, and God's love and mercy were all there for me to claim with the grace of Almighty God.

MacArthur also adds,

> Christ's teaching is clear: the person who believes he or she is spiritually safe without Him has no part in His kingdom. Our Lord came to earth to call sinners to repentance, but He cannot seek and save those who will not recognize they are lost—and the self-righteous need to re-examine their hearts concerning salvation before it's too late.[12]

Couple that with these comments he made in his book *Hard to Believe*:

> Let's make an important distinction between self-denial and penance. Self-denial is giving up creature comforts to work toward a worthy goal. Penance is self-punishment in hopes of earning God's favour, which is absolutely, 100 percent impossible—and 100 percent unnecessary. Not one can be good enough, or make himself feel bad enough, to earn his or her way into heaven. But no one has to, because Jesus paid the full price of entry on behalf of all true Christians.[13]

After many years of anxiety and making my way through life on my own, a sudden hope dawned on me. My marriage was just beginning, and at that point my life was looking good, at least from the world's point of view. But something was missing, and that void was about to be filled.

Paul moved on to a letter he wrote to the Ephesians. Although most translations say it's a letter to the Ephesians, some scholars believe, because the name Ephesus is not mentioned in every early manuscript, that this letter was to be circulated and read among all the churches. It may simply have been sent to the Ephesians first.

He told me in this letter that there is no way we can earn our way to heaven, and it's only by the grace of God that we can be saved.

Ephesians 2:8–9 says, *"For it is by grace you have been saved, through faith—and this not from yourselves, it is the gift of God—not by works, so that no one can boast."* This passage can be broken down into four categories: grace, faith, gift, and works.

It is true that if I had earned eternal life, I would have told everyone how it was done. This passage is one I would memorize and use over and over to remind myself that only Jesus saves!

Grace. *"For it is by grace you have been saved…"* The World's Bible Dictionary defines grace in the following way:

> There is much in the Bible about grace, partially because there is much in the Bible about sin. Grace is the undeserved favour of God. People repeatedly sin and rebel against God, yet God in His grace is still ready to forgive them when they repent. The only way people have ever been forgiven their sin and saved from condemnation is by grace, and they receive this salvation through faith.[14]

Warren Wiersbe adds,

> Grace means salvation completely apart from any merit or works on our part. Grace means that God does it all for Jesus' sake![15]

Faith. *"…through faith…"* In John 20:29, Jesus said, *"Because you have seen me, you have believed; blessed are those who have not seen and yet have believed."* That is real faith, as I have never seen Jesus, but I certainly believe is real and alive.

Hebrews 11:1 says, *"Now faith is confidence in what we hope for and assurance about what we do not see."* About this, Charles Ryrie wrote, "Faith gives reality and proof of things unseen, treating them as if they were already objects of sight rather than of hope."[16]

A good summary of Christian faith is found in *The New Illustrated Bible Dictionary*:

> *Faith is part of the Christian life from beginning to end. As the instrument by which the gift of salvation is received (Eph. 2:8–9), faith is thus distinct from the basis of salvation, which is grace, and from the outworking of salvation, which is good works. The apostle Paul declared that salvation is through faith, not through keeping the law (Gal. 2:16).*[17]

I would certainly have to take a step forward in faith. Honestly, it's not that big a step when you look around at creation. When you think of the earth and then add to it the vastness of the universe, you can see that we have a lot of visible evidence that something much greater than mankind put it all together. It doesn't take much faith to see this is not manmade.

Where did everything come from and how does it all work in harmony?

Gift. *"…it is the gift of God…"* For most people, this idea is difficult to comprehend. How could a holy, sinless God give us an opportunity to be granted the free gift of salvation?

The World's Bible Dictionary puts it this way: "God's salvation is not a reward for a person's faith; it is a free gift that no person in any way deserves, but they can receive it by faith."[18] William MacDonald adds,

> It is the gift of God. A gift of course is a free and unconditional present. That is the only basis on which God offers salvation. The gift of God is salvation by grace through faith. It is offered to all people everywhere.[19]

Today, everyone wants to earn their way to heaven. Many people have explained to me their plan: when they meet God, they will admit that they've done some things that were wrong, but overall they did their best to balance the scale on the side of good.

That is not at all what God is talking about. There's nothing we can do to earn our way into heaven.

I can't help but think of the scripture mentioned earlier in which people told Jesus all the things they were doing in His name, and He replied, *"Away from me, you evildoers!"* (Matthew 7:23) We need to rejoice in the incredible opportunity we have to claim the salvation of God as a free gift that cannot be earned. One of the main reasons it cannot be earned is because of the weakness of humanity and our inclination to boast.

Works. *"…not by works, so that no one can boast."* Boasting will continue to be an issue for me for many years to come, and I can see why Paul made it clear that my salvation has nothing to do with anything I can do of my own accord.

Can you imagine the stories people would tell about the great things they'd done to earn their way into the kingdom of God? No, we cannot earn our way into heaven by works. I'm not sure if the main reason is the incredible boasting that would occur if people were able to do this.

William MacDonald put it much more eloquently:

> If anyone could be saved by his own good works, then the death of Jesus was unnecessary. But we know that the reason He died was because there was no other way by which guilty sinners could be saved. If anyone could be saved by his own good works, then he would be his own saviour, and could worship himself. But this would be idolatry and God forbids it.[20]

2 Timothy 1:9 elaborates further: *"[Jesus] has saved us and called us to a holy life—not because of anything we have done but because of his own purpose and grace."*

The World's Bible Dictionary states,

> Confidence in self is one of the things that prevent people from coming to God and receiving God's salvation. People cannot earn salvation as a reward for any good deeds they might do. They can only receive it as a gift that God gives freely to those who trust in his grace. There is therefore nothing of themselves that they can boast about.[21]

We are now about to explore probably the most well-known verse in all of the New Testament. Certainly, it's one of the most important verses in Scripture, if not the most important. It is by far the most quoted verse, and usually the first one most Christians memorize. At major sporting events, you often see people holding up signs with a scripture on them, and most times it's this one.

I'll be devoting the next chapter to this verse since it's full of meanings and great promises, but for now we'll consider it in context with the Romans Road.

The verse is John 3:16, although I'll also be adding the following verse. In it, Jesus says,

> *For God so loved the world that he gave his one and only Son, that whoever believes in him shall not perish but have eternal life. For God did not send his Son into the world to condemn the world, but to save the world through him.*
> —John 3:16–17

This verse became the foundation and cornerstone of my faith. Having two sons of my own, I could never conceive of the notion of giving them up, let alone sending them to die for someone else. When you think about this verse, there are so many meanings and promises of hope and salvation in it—meanings and promises that could only come from God.

Charles Ryrie says,

> A new quality of life, not an everlasting "this life." Here begins another major theme of John: the dual one of redemption and judgement. Here the emphasis is on the fact that men judge themselves. The acquitted are those who have believed in Him; the condemned are those who have rejected Him.[22]

This was certainly what I wanted in my life, and Paul was about to show me how to achieve this eternal life. We're about to explore the way to salvation in Jesus Christ. The how-to of becoming a child of the King of Kings and Lord of Lords.

In Romans 10, Paul broke it down into three sections, showing the way in which people come to faith in Jesus.

Romans 10:9 says, "*If you declare with your mouth, 'Jesus is Lord,' and believe in your heart that God raised him from the dead, you will be saved.*"

In 1 Samuel 16:7, the Lord said to Samuel, "*The Lord does not look at the things people look at. People look at the outward appearance, but the Lord looks at the heart.*" You may make a public show of your faith and say all the right things, but you will never fool God. He goes directly for the heart and you can't mask that.

So this appears to be about more than saying a few words and feeling that you have done your duty to God.

In *Hard to Believe*, John MacArthur writes,

> Becoming a Christian means being sick of your sin, longing for forgiveness and rescue from the present evil and future hell, and affirming your commitment to the lordship of Christ to the point where you are willing to forsake everything. I've said it before, and I'll say it again; it isn't just holding up your hand or walking down an aisle and saying. "I love Jesus." It is not easy, it is not user-friendly or seeker sensitive, it isn't a rosy, perfect world where Jesus gives you whatever you want. It is hard, it is sacrificial, and it supersedes everything.[23]

This, in my estimation, is true Christianity.

Although I did walk forward at a Billy Graham crusade to dedicate my life to Jesus, that was only the beginning. Somewhere along life's journey, it becomes clear that following Jesus is not an easy road. It's a tough road. However, the joy you experience along the journey, coupled with the great confidence of living in anticipation of eternal life, is very much worth the trip. The joy of the Christian life is incredible, but it requires a heart change. John MacArthur wrote,

> This is a deep personal conviction, without reservation, that Jesus is God and the Lord of the universe. The phrase includes repenting from sin, trusting in Jesus for salvation and submitting to Him as Lord. This is vital to your faith.[24]

William MacDonald wrote in his Bible commentary,

> First—You must accept Jesus is the Lord of life and glory and the Lord of the Old Testament. Second—You must accept the truth of His resurrection. This is proof that Christ had completed the necessary work of salvation.[25]

As I continued to study God's Word, I realized that I had to *apply* these teachings to my life. If they were only words, with no action, what good would they be other than to tell a really good story? After reading and studying this verse, I found four applications:

1. Believe that Jesus is Lord.
2. Never lose sight of the importance of the Scriptures.
3. Submit to Jesus as Teacher and Lord.
4. Thank God daily for this remarkable gift!

Now there were actions I could associate with my studies. This made a tremendous change in my life with Jesus as I tried to live out the Bible. This was a game-changer!

Romans 10:10 says, *"For it is with your heart that you believe and are justified, and it is with your mouth that you profess your faith and are saved."*

Paul explained that this is the time to put some meat on your decision to meet the Lord Jesus on a personal level, establishing an actual relationship with the King of Kings. This is a magnificent passage, which states that words alone will not accomplish this; it must be a change of heart, mind, and soul.

My brother once said to me, "When you come to know Jesus as Saviour and Lord, there must be a difference in your life." You can't come to the throne of grace and walk away the same person.

> *Therefore, if anyone is in Christ, the new creation has come: The old has gone, the new is here!*
> —2 Corinthians 5:17

> *You were taught, with regard to your former way of life, to put off your old self, which is being corrupted by its deceitful desires; to be made new in the attitude of your minds; and to put on the new self, created to be like God in true righteousness and holiness.*
> —Ephesians 4:22–24

There must be evidence of a changed life; one's outlook needs to be based on eternal values rather than earthly gains.

Life as I knew it was never the same. I still faced many struggles, but the process of continual improvement had begun. During bumps in the road, another pivotal verse of Scripture I clung to was Philippians 1:6, which says, *"…being confident of this, that he who began a good work in you will carry it on to completion until the day of Christ Jesus."* I developed confidence in my new life in Jesus.

The next section of the Romans Road discusses verbal confession since this is about more than merely making a decision within your heart. Romans 1:16 says, *"For I am not ashamed of the gospel, because it is the power of God that brings salvation to everyone who believes…"*

Adding to this, Jesus stated in Matthew 10:32–33, *"Whoever acknowledges me before others, I will also acknowledge before my Father in heaven. But whoever disowns me before others, I will disown before my Father in heaven."*

Charles Ryrie writes, "There are simultaneous actions; one inward (heart), and the other outward (mouth)."[26] William MacDonald also made a great observation about this passage:

> A heart believing unto righteousness, and a mouth making confession unto salvation, are not really two things, but two sides of the same thing. First, you believe, then you make a public confession of salvation. The believer publicly confesses the salvation he has already received. Confession is not a condition of salvation but the inevitable outward expression of what happened. When a person really believes something, he wants to share it with others. So, when a person is genuinely born again, it is too good to keep secret. He confesses Christ.[27]

I had to take certain steps when this verse became real in my life. After review, these are the applications I wanted to put into practice:

1. Tell others about Jesus.
2. Realize that God knows your heart, no matter what you may say.
3. Live a righteous life, with the help of Jesus, and tell others about the joy that comes from the salvation of Jesus.

Romans 10:13 says, *"Everyone who calls on the name of the Lord will be saved."* Paul explains that salvation is wonderful and there is reason for those who are saved to feel special, but this experience isn't unique to us as individuals; God loved the world so much that He opened this experience to everyone. He didn't say that everyone *would* be saved, but He said that everyone who calls upon the Lord will be saved. As it states in John 3:16–17,

> *For God so loved the world that he gave his one and only Son, that whoever believes in him shall not perish but have eternal life. For God did not send his Son into the world to condemn the world, but to save the world through him.*

What an incredible offering from the Creator of the universe! How could anyone say no to this?

I came to learn that this becomes an issue of Lordship. People seem open to having Jesus save them from hell, but not to become Lord of their lives. This is where things become complicated for people. It is one thing to receive Jesus as Saviour, but it's another thing altogether for Him to become Lord of your life; this is where you turn everything over to Him. The deep, deep love of God and incredible mercy and grace that caused Him to send His Son to die in our place is inconceivable.

And yet people prefer the here and now. This goes back to the wide gate that leads to destruction. What a tragedy it is for people to think the temporal pleasure of this world will satisfy, leaving them to prefer that over Jesus.

I've always said there are three killers in a relationship, work, parenting, or anything else in life: pride, arrogance, and unaccountability. It's a tough decision to lay down your life and all your possessions when you're living for the here and now.

This is what it means to call upon the name of the Lord Jesus first and foremost. Everything else follows from that decision. This is what Jesus meant when he said in the Sermon on the Mount, *"But seek first his kingdom and his righteousness, and all these things will be given to you as well"* (Matthew 6:33).

There are three applications for this verse:

1. Call upon the name of the Lord.
2. Never forget that you have been saved through faith.
3. Praise God daily for His path to salvation.

Now that I've been born again and become a child of the Most High God, it was time for me to live a life that honoured the Lord Jesus Christ. I expressed my sincere gratitude to Paul for our travels down the Romans Road.

However, he said to me, "We're not finished. Now that you have the free gift of God with Jesus as your Lord and Saviour, what do you plan to do with it? We have two more verses to cover to begin the new life in Christ."

Paul then explained that you have to give your life fully to Jesus. To do this, He sent the Holy Spirit as a helper to direct your life and pierce your conscience when you're being led astray. Eventually, this spiritual prodding becomes a natural part of your life as a Christian.

As you do things the way you used to, you'll feel a nudge or prodding to turn away and go in a different direction. God has set up a way for you to improve on this day by day as you grow in your walk with Jesus.

Now we come to the last two verses in the Romans Road, which will move you further in that direction.

Romans 12:1 says, *"Therefore, I urge you, brothers and sisters, in view of God's mercy, to offer your bodies as a living sacrifice, holy and pleasing to God—this is your true and proper worship."*

Now is the time to show God that you're taking this life seriously. In the Old Testament, there were different sacrifices for different sins. Can you imagine today if someone had to carry out a burnt offering every time they sinned? There would be fires on every property continually! What a visual aid that would be, if our sins were brought front and centre for all the world to see.

Thankfully, Jesus paid the sacrifice once and for all on the cross of Calvary.

But now was the time for me to respond in my own manner—not as a dead sacrifice but as a living sacrifice.

Living a righteous life doesn't look like self-service, but rather an act of worship to God that pleases Him. Rather than attempting to do something above and beyond, it should become my way of life—not in order to get something, but to live in thankfulness. This is something that would take a lifetime to learn, but with the help of the Holy Spirit, it's a process of continual improvement.

1 Peter 1:14 says, *"As obedient children, do not conform to the evil desires you had when you lived in ignorance."* Paul also confirms this in 1 Corinthians 6:19–20:

> *Do you not know that your bodies are temples of the Holy Spirit, who is in you, whom you have received from God? You are not your own; you were bought at a price. Therefore honor God with your bodies.*

William MacDonald wrote, "Our bodies stand for all our members and by extension our entire lives. Total commitment is our reasonable service."[28]

There is an old hymn called that says, "Love so amazing, so divine, demands my soul, my life, my all."[29] This is an all-in life, not part-time.

I came up with two applications based on these ideas:

1. Live a life that honours God and pleases Him.
2. Thank God daily for His mercy and grace, and worship Him.

Romans 12:2 says, "*Do not conform to the pattern of this world, but be transformed by the renewing of your mind. Then you will be able to test and approve what God's will is—his good, pleasing and perfect will.*"

Paul explained that this idea is crucial to developing a strong walk with the Lord. Things in my life would have to change, and the only way to do this was to change my habits through the things I did and said.

Paul stated that this would be a lifelong journey, a marathon and not a sprint. It started with the things that were entering my mind through my eyes and ears. What was I listening to, watching, and reading? It didn't take long for me to conclude that I wasn't putting good and wholesome things into my mind.

I once saw an incredible motivational speaker named Zig Ziglar who said, "If you dump garbage in, garbage will come out. The person who dumps garbage into your mind will do you considerably more harm than the one who dumps garbage on your floor."[30] That's when I stopped reading the newspaper or listening to the news. It was all bad! Murder, robbery, rape, war, economic crises… there was nothing good in the news. Please don't misunderstand—I think it is important to be informed, but the news can quickly mesmerize us and become the focal point of our attention.

Romans 12:2 speaks about renewing your mind and thinking about heavenly things, the positive things that come only from God. The love of Jesus should be paramount in my thinking, as well as the incredible gift of forgiveness of sin and realizing that my name is written in heaven! That is exciting! That is the good news of the gospel.

Charles Ryrie wrote, "Do not live according to the style or manner of the present age. A continual process of change from the inside out. Dedication gives you the ability to discern God's will."[31]

1 John 2:15–17 expands on this idea further:

> *Do not love the world or anything in the world. If anyone loves the world, love for the Father is not in them. For everything in the world—the lust of the flesh, the lust of the eyes, and the pride of life—comes not from the Father but from the world. The world and its desires pass away, but whoever does the will of God lives forever.*

It seemed that almost everything I was living for was based on the applause of people or other self-serving purposes. Boasting has been a lifelong struggle for me and I pray that God will teach me to continue to honour and glorify Him.

John MacArthur breaks down some significant concepts in this verse:

> CONFORM: refers to assuming an outward expression that does not reflect what is really inside, a kind of masquerade or art. The word implies that Paul's readers were already allowing this to happen and must stop.
>
> WORLD: Better translated "age" which refers to the system of beliefs, values—or the spirit of the age—at any time current in the world. The sum of contemporary thinking and values form the moral atmosphere of our world and is always dominated by Satan.
>
> TRANSFORM: Christians should outwardly manifest their inner redeemed nature, not once, however but daily. All this will create Holy living in which God approves.
>
> RENEWAL: That kind of transformation can occur only as the Holy Spirit changes our thinking through constant study and meditation of Scripture.[32]

William MacDonald sums it up: "Don't let the world around you squeeze you into its own mould. Three keys to knowing God's will; yielded body, separated life and transformed mind."[33]

Three applications came to mind based on 1 John 2:15–17.

1. Spend time and study the Word of God regularly.
2. Never let a day go by without reading God's Word.
3. When worldly thoughts creep in, pray and study.

Going forward, I hope to introduce you to many people from the Bible and demonstrate how their stories directed my life and helped me to handle every situation that came my way. The Word of God is an incredible book that was written as a guide for us, and I hope to show you how you can use it daily in your own journey.

- Chapter Five -

John 3:16

As mentioned earlier, John 3:16 is the most well-known verse in the Bible, memorized and recited by many Christians. When I met John on my journey through the Scriptures, he explained that John 3:16 was part of a passage describing a conversation between Jesus and a Pharisee named Nicodemus, a high-ranking religious figure and member of the Sanhedrin, the highest ruling body and court of justice among the Jewish people. This was a serious religious leader coming to Jesus discreetly in the night.

We won't focus on the entire conversation, but this is where the term *"born again"* (John 3:3) first appears. Our time will mostly be spent on the later parts of the discussion.

So many ideas are built into this verse that volumes could be written about it.

First, we need to know more about the author, John. Who is he? Let's look into the background of the apostle known as *"the one Jesus loved"* (John 20:2).

I asked John to tell me about himself so I could get to know him better. Considering he spent years with Jesus, this is someone I wanted to understand!

"I was the son of a fisherman named Zebedee, and me and my brother James followed our dad into the family business," he explained. "James and I had a nickname back in those days: the Sons of Thunder. We were a very tough pair to deal with, and at one point, in anger, we asked Jesus to call down fire on some specific individuals. We were also extremely self-centred, to the point that we both made requests through our mom to have seats of honour with Jesus when He set up His kingdom. When Peter joined us, he was another aggressive, straightforward individual."

As I learned more, I immediately thought, *Jesus chose some fairly able men to be in His inner circle!*

"James and I were on the road to self-destruction," John added. "Who knows how this story would have ended had we not met Jesus?"

When you think of where John came from, his transformation is nothing short of miraculous. He became someone who was strong but gentle, straightforward but loving, and courageous but humble. There's no other way to account for this other than the influence of Jesus, being accepted and loved and affirmed by God and being filled with the Holy Spirit. What a change he went through from someone who had been desperate for power and recognition!

John was so overwhelmed with Jesus that he never mentions his own name in the book he himself wrote. He transformed from a Son of Thunder into the Apostle of Love! This is the transformation I needed in my life. Surrendering everything to Jesus is easy to talk about, but it takes a lifetime to achieve.

I asked John to tell me a little bit more about the book that bears his name.

"All Scripture is God-breathed," he said. "I may have written it, but the Holy Spirit moved the pen. Still, I wrote the book between 85–90 AD, and I was honoured when Jesus started identifying me as the apostle He loved. The book was written to the church and the theme centred on the reality of Jesus as God. Almost half of the words written in this book are spoken by Jesus. I presented Jesus as the divine Son of God, with the inspiration of the Holy Spirit."

As we've already seen, John 3:16 states, *"For God so loved the world that he gave his one and only Son, that whoever believes in him shall not perish but have eternal life."* It's such a short verse with such enormous meaning and hope. There are twelve great affirmations mentioned in this verse:

> For God (the greatest lover) so loved (the greatest degree) the world (the greatest number) that he gave (the greatest act) his one and only Son (the greatest gift), that whoever (the

greatest invitation) believes (the greatest simplicity) in him (the greatest person) shall not perish (the greatest escape) but (the greatest difference) have (the greatest certainty) eternal life (the greatest destiny).[34]

What an extensive list of blessings contained within just one verse of God's Word! Let's review each section of this passage and unpack its meaning to see the depth and love of God expressed through Jesus Christ.

For God (the greatest lover). *Vine's Complete Expository Dictionary* notes,

> God comes from the Greek noun "theos." Hence the word was appropriated by Jews and retained by Christians to denote "the one true God." In the Septuagint, "theos" translates (with few exceptions) the Hebrew words Elohim and Jehovah, the former indicating His power and pre-eminence, the latter His unoriginated immutable, eternal and self-sustained existence.[35]

In this verse, we truly see God as the greatest lover, because this is not just for a certain group of individuals—it is offered to the world at large.

It's hard to fathom God's ways. He is the Creator of the universe, but He loves individuals, like a father loves a child. He is everywhere and is everything. Psalm 8:4 asks, "[W]hat is mankind that you are mindful of them?" Though each person is insignificant compared to the stupendous work of creation, God cares for each of us as individuals!

The love of God cannot be compared to any love we have ever experienced. Couple this with the fact that we are dealing with the Most High God. The way we look at God when we think of Him should be mirrored in the way the Bible tells us to pray when referring to Him: "*Our Father in heaven, hallowed by your name*" (Matthew 6:9). Always take the time to hallow the name of the Creator God, and never take for granted our greatest Lover.

So loved (the greatest degree). Here John is talking about the depth of God's love. *Vine's* explains that the word "love" spoken here comes from the Greek verb *agapao*, and the corresponding noun *agape*.[36]

The New Illustrated Bible Dictionary tells us that this type of love is the characteristic word of Christianity.[37] It indicates the nature of the love of God toward His beloved Son (John 17:26), toward the human race generally (John 3:16), and toward those who believe on the Lord Jesus Christ (John 14:21).

Now we can see the greatest degree of love that could only come from God.

Love is so much the dominating characteristic of the divine nature that the Bible declares simply that God *is* love. Everything God says or does is in some way an expression of love. 1 John 4:8 says, "*Whoever does not love does not know God, because God is love.*" In the same chapter, we read, "*And so we know and rely on the love God has for us. God is love. Whoever lives in love lives in God, and God in him*" (John 4:16).

We are looked upon as God's children. Love can be known by its action, and this is not a love we deserve. As Romans 5:8 explains, "*While we were still sinners, Christ died for us.*"

Christian love, whether expressed toward Christians or non-Christians, is generally not based on an emotional impulse. As a Christian, we are called to love others. It is the type of love that seeks the welfare of all and does no evil to anyone; it seeks opportunity to do good to all, especially other Christians.

As Christians, we are to do what is good and righteous. Ephesians 2:10 says, "*For we are God's handiwork, created in Christ Jesus to do good works, which God prepared in advance for us to do.*" This is not a form of salvation by works, but the heart's reaction to Jesus's residence within you.

When we show God's love to others, great things will happen. Ephesians 2:4–5 says, "*But because of his great love for us, God, who is rich in mercy, made us alive with Christ even when we were dead in transgressions—it is by grace you have been saved.*"

I am thankful that Jesus loved me so much that He died on the cross, and I am amazed that God loved me to the greatest degree. How can we not show love to others when God showed this degree of love toward us?

The world (the greatest number). The word "world" comes from the Greek noun *kosmos*, meaning the earth as in contrast to heaven. It also includes the people who inhabit the earth.

This verse does not speak about God's love of the physical planet, but rather the people who live there. Therefore, He is reaching the greatest number that it is possible to reach.

Because of sin, the world has become a place where Satan rules in people's lives. Therefore, the Bible frequently speaks of the present world—this present age—as something that is evil and opposed to God.

The entire world has been bitten by sin. Paul wrote that *"all have sinned and fall short of the glory of God"* (Romans 3:23) and *"the wages of sin is death"* (Romans 6:23). God sent His Son to die not only for Israel but for the whole world.

One of the many things I love about the Christian faith is that God extended His saving grace to everyone on the planet. Think about it: the God of the universe loved us so much that He opened salvation to the whole world—not just parts or groups, but to everyone who would trust in Jesus as their Lord and Saviour. Incredible! The earth will pass away, but the person who does the will of God lives forever.

That He gave (the greatest act). When I hear the word *act*, I think of live theatre; there are several acts in a play. After the play, some may discuss which was their favourite act.

Over the years, there have been many great plays, and many great acts, but none like this act! The act we're talking about is the greatest act ever. God Himself gave something that could not be given by anyone else, and the sacrifice is too great to comprehend or put into words. It's an enormous act of giving.

Collins English Dictionary defines the word "give" in the following way: "to present or deliver voluntarily (something that is one's own) to another."[38]

The greatest act is this gift of God (Romans 6:23), given to mankind to pay for our sins. We should never feel proud that we deserved this gift, but rather we should be incredibly humble. Romans 10:13 says, *"Everyone who calls upon the name of the Lord will be saved."*

Romans 8:31–32 talks about giving:

What then, shall we say in response to this? If God is for us, who can stand against us? He who did not spare his own Son but gave

Him up for us all—how will He not also, along with Him graciously give us all things?

Twice in this verse, variations of the word "give" are used, which reveals that this is by far the greatest act. Our goal in life should be to express this greatest act to others through the giving of our resources and time.

This message needs to be shared with others. God, grant me the courage to tell others about this great performance or act of love.

His one and only Son (the greatest gift). The King James Version of the Bible uses the term *"only begotten,"* which comes from the Greek word *monogenes*. With reference to Jesus, this indicates that He, as the Son of God, was the sole representative of the being and character of the One who sent Him. Jesus became God incarnate—that is, He took upon Himself human form.

You can see that the word "begotten" changes the entire meaning of the verse. When you think of the way in which Jesus was born through the virgin Mary, He surely had to be the One and Only. This is by far the greatest gift that could possibly be given.

In being a man, Jesus didn't cease to be God. His deity was not lessened in any way. Jesus had existed as God throughout eternity, yet He willingly sacrificed the supreme glory of heaven and took instead the place of a servant. What He sacrificed was not his deity, but the heavenly glories that were His by right.

This was God in the flesh. As John 1:14 says, *"The Word became flesh and made his dwelling among us."*[39] And Philippians 2:5–7 adds,

> *In your relationships with one another, have the same mindset as Christ Jesus: who, being in very nature God, did not consider equality with God something to be used to his own advantage; rather, he made himself nothing by taking the very nature of a servant, being made in human likeness.*

This unmistakably states that Jesus Christ was God in the flesh. May I never forget this great sacrifice He made for mankind. I should thank God daily for the salvation He provided.

That whoever (the greatest invitation). In the King James Version, the word "whoever" is substituted for the word "whosoever," which is based on the Greek word *pas*, meaning "all." This truly is the greatest invitation.

God does not have an exclusive invitation list; Jesus died for everyone. Colossians 3:11 explains, *"Here there is no Gentile or Jew, circumcised or uncircumcised, barbarian, Scythian, slave or free, but Christ is all, and is in all."* And in Romans 10:12–13, we read, *"For there is no difference between Jew and Gentile—the same Lord is Lord of all and richly blesses all who call on him, for, 'Everyone who calls on the name of the Lord will be saved.'"*

Further in Romans, Paul writes, *"This righteousness is given through faith in Jesus Christ to all who believe. There is no difference between Jew and Gentile, for all have sinned and fall short of the glory of God"* (Romans 3:22–23). This last one is a great verse to share with someone who feels they've committed too many wrongs to ever make things right. In one's own power, it is impossible to be made right before God, but nothing is impossible for Him.

Being part of the family of God is a great way to live, but we need to make sure we share this with everyone we possibly can.

I am very thankful that my mom took the time to tell me about Jesus. His family is wide open, ready to embrace anyone who repents of their sins and comes to Jesus. Eternal life is an incredible gift to receive!

Just think of all the parties or social events that you didn't receive an invitation to. Well, once you fall on your knees before Jesus and receive Him as Lord and Saviour, the invitation will not be rescinded—you will be a member forever.

Believes (the greatest simplicity). The word "believe" used in this passage comes from the Greek verb *pisteuo*, which means "to be persuaded of" and hence "to place confidence in, to trust."[40] John explained that he used the word "believe" most frequently in his writing, especially in his gospel. Matthew used the verb ten times, Mark used it ten times, and Luke used it nine times. But John used it ninety-nine times. We can see that this truly was the theme of John's Gospel.

Believing is more than just entering into an intellectual agreement that Jesus is God. It means putting our trust and confidence in Him and accepting that He alone can save us. It is to put the Lord Jesus Christ in charge of our present plans and eternal destiny. Believing means both trusting His words as reliable and relying on Him for the power to change.

John 3:18 says, "*Whoever believes in him is not condemned, but whoever does not believe stands condemned already because they have not believed in the name of God's one and only Son.*" From this passage, it's clear that I need to identify what I believe and where to put my trust and confidence. I put it in the Lord Jesus Christ. This truth is truly the greatest simplicity.

In Him (the greatest person). The "him" in this verse comes from the Greek noun *autos*, which means "he, himself, no other."[41] The word was used frequently in John's Gospel, as well as in Revelation. It's also, of course, a reference to Jesus, the Son of God, God in the flesh.

There is no doubt in my mind that the term "greatest person" fits the Lord Jesus Christ. There is a great passage in the book of Hebrews that not only defines Jesus but shows His incredible love and understanding for us. The plan and process God has given to those who believe in the Lord Jesus is truly amazing. Hebrews 4:14–16 says,

> *Therefore, since we have a great high priest who has ascended into heaven, Jesus the Son of God, let us hold firmly to the faith we profess. For we do not have a high priest who is unable to empathize with our weaknesses, but we have one who has been tempted in every way, just as we are—yet he did not sin. Let us then approach God's throne of grace with confidence, so that we may receive mercy and find grace to help us in our time of need.*

It is amazing to realize that the God of the universe sent His Son to earth not only to die for our sins but also fully grasp what we go through on earth. He was tempted just as we are and knows the ways of the world. He not only talks the talk but has walked the walk. I must never forget that there is no one in history like Jesus. It's all about Him.

Shall not perish (the greatest escape). During the Second World War, a group of Allied soldiers became known for their ability to break out of prison. Therefore, when they were captured, they were confined to an escape-proof prison camp. A movie was made about these men in 1963, called *The Great Escape*.

In the movie, only a few soldiers managed to escape their confinement. That's the difference between the movie and the escape provided by God. The men caught in the movie were sent back to prison or died. But we are free forever. Our chains have been broken, our sin forgiven! Our escape is guaranteed and there is no turning back. Through the Lord Jesus's death and resurrection, we truly experience the greatest escape.

To word "perish" comes from the Greek word *apollumi*, meaning to destroy. In this context, it refers to the death of a person. Another dictionary defines this word to mean "to be destroyed or die, especially in an untimely way."[42]

We will all die eventually, but Jesus accepted our punishment and paid the price for our sins so that we would not perish. Honestly, we should read that sentence again and again!

In this verse, Jesus isn't referring to our physical death. When He talks about perishing, He means spending eternity apart from God. However, we who believe have an alternative. Praise God for this hope and promise! There is no need for anyone to perish.

A way has been provided by which all might be saved, but we must acknowledge the Lord Jesus Christ as our personal Saviour. The difference between perishing and living, between condemnation and salvation, is having faith in Jesus Christ. Jesus could well have come to this world as a Judge, destroying every rebellious sinner, but He instead came to the world in love, as Saviour, and died for us on the cross. As John 3:17 tells us, *"For God did not send his Son into the world to condemn the world, but to save the world through him."*

There can be no doubt that this is the greatest escape in history. Praise God.

But (the great difference) have (the greatest certainty) eternal life (the greatest destiny). The last three portions of this passage reveal some amazing truths.

The first word is "but," an incredible three-letter word. As you read through Scripture, you will see it used again and again. This one follows the word "perish," and what a great relief it is to know that there is a "but" right after the word "perish." Can you imagine if a period followed "perish"? Even better are the two words preceding it: "shall not." So we are not going to perish.

The "but" here then leads into the next small word: "have." What a huge impact these two small words can have on your life. Together, they form the greatest difference and greatest certainty.

This leads us, finally, to eternal life, our greatest destiny. The word "eternal," or "everlasting," comes from the Greek word *aionois*. In this case, the meaning refers to persons and things that are in nature endless.[43]

John 3:15 tells us *"that everyone who believes may have eternal life in him."* John MacArthur, referring to this verse, writes,

> This is the first of 17 references to "eternal life" in John's Gospel. The expression appears in the New Testament nearly 50 times. Eternal life refers not only to eternal quantity, but also divine quality of life. It means literally, "life of the age to come" and refers therefore to resurrection and heavenly existence in perfect glory and holiness.
>
> This life for believers in the Lord Jesus is experienced even before heaven is reached. The "eternal life," is in essence nothing less than participation in the eternal life of the Living Word, Jesus Christ. It is the life of God in every believer, yet not fully manifest until the resurrection.[44]

The example given to us in John 3:16 tells of the life which is received by those who believe in Christ, who will never perish.

There are two eternities mentioned by Jesus. The first is from Matthew 25:46: *"Then they will go away to eternal punishment, but the righteous to eternal life."* Just before raising Lazarus from the dead, Jesus then spoke of this to Lazarus's sister Martha:

> *Jesus said to her, "I am the resurrection and the life. The one who believes in me will live, even though they die; and whoever lives by believing in me will never die. Do you believe this?"*

> "Yes, Lord," she replied, "I believe that you are the Messiah, the Son of God, who is to come into the world."
>
> —John 11:25–27

We will never die, neither spiritually nor eternally. We have the new life Jesus bought for us, which is everlasting life with God!

While concluding this chapter, I've come up with three applications:

1. Live your life certain of eternal life with God.
2. Do not worry about things of this world. God is in control.
3. Live your life to the fullest for Jesus!

I took a moment to thank John for walking me through one of the greatest Bible verses ever written. I looked forward to meeting him again as I journeyed through the Bible.

- Chapter Six -
Psalm 15

It seems that I say the same thing about every passage of Scripture, but this is one of my all-time favourites. It's very difficult to pull out almost any passage and not feel that way, once you study it and discover its origins, themes, and message. That is why the Bible is one of the most incredible books ever written!

Sunday after Sunday, as our pastor introduces the Scripture for the message, I find myself saying to myself, "I love this passage!" That's probably the best explanation I could ever give to God's Word: "I love this Book!"

It is my hope that everyone who reads this chapter will want to become a "Psalm 15 person." This is my life's goal: that one day I can confidently say that I am a Psalm 15 man. Honestly, if anyone could live these verses after receiving Jesus as Lord and Saviour, their life would be complete.

The psalm finishes with an incredible promise: *"Whoever does these things will never be shaken"* (Psalm 15:5). What a promise!

Now, let's dig deeply into the verses and find out what the criteria are to become a Psalm 15 person.

Over the past few years of my life, I've had the privilege of leading a discipling community group at our local church. I was given a group of eight Grade Ten students. Needless to say, I was much older than these guys.

When the youth leader asked me to do this, my immediate response was, "Oh, this can't miss. An old guy teaching Grade Ten students!" Well, he asked me to pray about it and I did—and I eventually took the class.

I kept thinking to myself, *How am I going to relate to these fifteen-year-olds?* In my life, I had run a division of a company, spoke publicly to large groups, chaired the elders' board of a large church, and attended many tough meetings in boardrooms. I say this to confirm that I had never been so nervous about a meeting than I was the first night I met these eight young men.

The first night, I showed up in a room with a table and nine chairs. One by one, they filed into the room. I just sat there, not sure what to say as all the young men greeted each other—they had been friends for years and I certainly wasn't part of the inner circle.

Amidst the noise of their chatter, I finally asked, "Why are you guys here?" The room immediately became deadly silent and I waited for what seemed like forever.

"To learn about God," one of them said at last, and they all nodded in agreement.

"Okay," I said. "That's your parents' answer. But why are *you* here?" No one spoke, so I continued. "You all rated your last leader very highly. I assume he did a great job?"

"Yes, we had a lot of fun," another of them said.

"Excellent. Give me three life lessons you learned."

At that point, you could have heard a pin drop. No one said anything. It was at that point that I realized it wasn't that they'd had a bad leader, but that it's exceedingly difficult to get Grade Ten students to participate in group discussion. It's easy to get frustrated.

Finally, I said, "Would you like to know what keeps a guy like me awake at night?"

They were all ears at this point and I truly felt that I had their complete attention. They seemed genuinely interested in knowing the answer.

"Where did all the men go?" I asked. "There doesn't appear to be many men who stand up for what is right. If you take a stand on almost anything, people say you are a bigot; if you are a Christian and you take a stand, people think you are a fool. My hope is that when this time with you guys is over, I want to ask, where did all the men go? And my prayer is that all of you will raise your hand and say, 'Right here!' Are you guys interested in participating in this?"

I almost fell off my chair when they all enthusiastically replied, "Yes!"

At that point, I felt that God had me exactly where He wanted me. What happened over the next three years with these young men was incredible, and I will always thank God for letting me participate in this amazing group.

Why did I tell you this story? The basis and foundation of our group became Psalm 15. One of the first of many challenges I gave these young men was to memorize it. Once they completed this task, they would receive a study Bible, commentary, and dictionary. All of them completed this in record time. Now they had the tools to study the Word of God.

So let's take a look at Psalm 15:

Lord, who may dwell in your sacred tent? Who may live on your holy mountain? The one whose walk is blameless, who does what is righteous, who speaks the truth from their heart; whose tongue utters no slander, who does no wrong to a neighbor, and casts no slur on others; who despises a vile person but honors those who fear the Lord; who keeps an oath even when it hurts, and does not change their mind; who lends money to the poor without interest; who does not accept a bribe against the innocent. Whoever does these things will never be shaken.

—Psalm 15:1–5

As you can see, it takes a very short time to read this psalm, but I can assure you that it takes a lifetime to live it. I'm reminded of Philippians 1:6, which says, *"being confident of this, that he who began a good work in you will carry it on to completion until the day of Christ Jesus."* This is a great verse of hope, especially for type-A personalities who think they'll conquer this in no time.

It's important to realize this isn't a chapter about working your way into heaven. That can only happen by receiving Jesus as your Lord and Saviour. Once that has happened, you will want to change your life for the better and do good works, as God said to Christians in Ephesians 2:10: *"For we are God's handiwork, created in Christ Jesus to do good works, which God prepared in advance for us to do."* William MacDonald adds,

> The individual God chooses as His companion is the subject of Psalm 15. Although it does not say so in the Psalm, the

basic qualification for entrance into God's kingdom is to be born again. Apart from the new birth, no one can see or enter the kingdom. The birth from above is experienced by grace, through faith, and takes place completely apart from any meritorious words on the man's part.[45]

Further, James 4:17 says, *"If anyone, then, knows the good they ought to do and doesn't do it, it is sin for them."*

The first thing we need to do is research the background of this psalm before we take it apart verse by verse. So it's time to meet David.

Background. David began by telling me some stories from his long and interesting life. The most widely known event David is remembered for is his encounter with Goliath.

"It was a normal day for me, as I was looking after the sheep I had in my charge," he told me. "But before I tell you about Goliath, let me tell you about shepherding sheep. I'm amazed at not only what I learned during this time, but how dangerous this job truly was. People usually don't equate sheepherding with danger, but believe me, it can be dangerous! Twice I encountered dangerous animals. One day I was tending the sheep when suddenly a lion and a bear came on the scene and attempted to kill my flock. Thankfully, I was able to defend against the predators as the Lord watched over me."

He then moved on to his encounter with Goliath.

"The Philistine army was on one side of a valley and the Israelite army was on the other," David explained. "Goliath was a giant from Gath who stood taller than any other soldier and was taunting the Israelite army to send their toughest soldier to fight him, with the winner being granted the right to rule. No one would go against Goliath. However, one day I showed up to bring some food to the soldiers and saw what was happening. I was immediately filled with righteous anger that someone would do this to God's army."

As it states in 1 Samuel 17:34–37,

But David said to Saul, "Your servant used to keep sheep for his father. And when there came a lion, or a bear, and took a lamb

> *from the flock, I went after him and struck him and delivered it out of his mouth. And if he arose against me, I caught him by his beard and struck him and killed him. Your servant has struck down both lions and bears, and this uncircumcised Philistine shall be like one of them, for he has defied the armies of the living God." And David said, "The Lord who delivered me from the paw of the lion and from the paw of the bear will deliver me from the hand of this Philistine." And Saul said to David, "Go, and the Lord be with you!"* (ESV)

Can you imagine David, an unarmed boy, going into the valley against a huge man with full armour, waiting to annihilate him?

Well, we know how the story ends. David defeats Goliath with a slingshot and a stone, and his fame began to grow. He went on to become the anointed king, and though he encountered some major setbacks in life, his bloodline would eventually produce Jesus, and God would call him *"a man after his own heart"* (1 Samuel 13:14).

David wrote seventy-three of the one hundred fifty psalms, one of which being Psalm 15. Charles Ryrie, in his commentary of Psalm 15, wrote,

> Here David describes the character of the person who qualifies to be a guest of God. The synonymous, parallel questions of verse 1 are answered in the following verses by an elevenfold description of the righteous man who is upright in deed, work, attitude, and finances. These qualities, not natural to men, are imparted by God.[46]

Warren Wiersbe said,

> The rabbis taught that there were 613 commandments for the Jewish people to obey if they wanted to be righteous, but this psalm brings the number down to eleven.[47] Isaiah 33:15–16 gives six requirements, and Micah 6:8 lists three. Habakkuk 2:4 names but one–faith–for faith in Jesus Christ is the only

way to have your sins forgiven and be welcomed into the Lord's presence.[48]

Psalm 15:1 says, *"Lord, who may dwell in your sacred tent? Who may live on your holy mountain?"*
Observation. David said he wanted to know from God what type of people He would like to fellowship with—or, in modern lingo, "hang out" with. Here's a great question we should constantly ask ourselves: is what I am doing right now something God would want to join?

John MacArthur explains that the psalm begins with a two-part question (15:1), and is followed by a twelve-part response (15:2–5), concluding with a one-part guarantee (15:5). I think this is an excellent overview of this psalm!

William MacDonald says,

> Taken by itself, the psalm seems to imply that salvation is somehow connected with a man's righteous character or noble deeds. But taken with the rest of Scripture, it can only mean that the kind of faith that saves is the same kind of faith that results in a life of holiness. Like James in his epistle, David is here saying that genuine faith in the Lord results in the kind of good works described in this psalm.[49]

Application. There are two applications that can be taken from this:

1. Before doing anything else, ask yourself the two questions in Psalm 15:1.
2. Understand that God knows everything.

Psalm 15:2 says, *"The one whose walk is blameless, who does what is righteous, who speaks the truth from their heart."*
Observation. When the words "blameless" and "righteous" are used in the original language, they mean "mature" or "well-rounded," though not sinless. Psalm 18:32 says, *"It is God who arms me with strength and makes my way secure."*

As William MacDonald stated, "You can depend on this man to tell the truth from his heart. He would rather die than lie. His word is his bond. His yes means yes and his no means no."[50]

I would often tell my family, as well as people in business, that I would take the word of my dad over any contract written by a high-priced lawyer. When you shook my dad's hand, you could take it to the bank. This may be a little self-serving, but I want to believe—and have been told by many business partners—that I inherited this trait from my dad. I always valued my word. It was my bond.

This short verse has so many meanings, as does this entire psalm. As I said at the beginning of this chapter, after receiving your saving faith from the Lord Jesus, if you could live according to this psalm, your life would be close to complete. Warren Wiersbe sums it up this way:

> If we are right in these basic virtues, we will "work them out" in every area of life and be obedient to the Lord. "Walk," "work" and "speak" are action words indicating the dedicated believer is constantly obeying the Lord and seeking to please Him.[51]

John MacArthur lists three positive ethical characteristics from this verse:

1. His lifestyle exhibits integrity.
2. His deeds exhibit justice.
3. His speech exhibits reliability.[52]

When you first look at Psalm 15:2 and see these three words—blameless, righteous, and truth—they seem to cover almost every area of your life. Consider these three words in school, your marriage, and your career in terms of living a life that honours our Lord Jesus. In anything we do or say, these words play a role.

This is why I love the Bible; three words can be life-changing. Imagine receiving Jesus as Lord and Saviour and spending the rest of your life living these three words. Amazing!

Application. There are three applications to be mined from this verse:

1. Do not lie.
2. Live a life of integrity and justice with the help of the Holy Spirit.
3. Leaning totally on Jesus, live a blameless and righteous life.

Psalm 15:3 says, "...*whose tongue utters no slander, who does no wrong to a neighbor, and casts no slur on others.*" This verse demonstrates the positive aspects of the person David was writing about, but we don't get into the negative side of their life.

Although this book was written some two thousand years ago, this verse is relevant for today and is full of constructive wisdom and advice for living a godly life.

How many times in my life have I contributed to conversations of a negative nature, doing so under the false pretences of caring for the individual? No matter how you justify it, this type of talk makes you a slanderer.

People tend to tear others down in order to build themselves up. The words "neighbour" and "fellow man" cover everyone you cross paths with. Anyone you communicate with falls into this category. I hate to say it, but this also includes family members talking about other family members, co-workers talking about other co-workers, students talking about other students, and worst of all, Christians talking about other Christians. This includes the scenario where you come home from church and serve up the pastor's sermon for lunch as you tear it apart.

James 3:10 says, "*Out of the same mouth come praise and cursing. My brothers and sisters, this should not be.*" Ephesians 4:29 says, "*Do not let any unwholesome talk come out of your mouths, but only what is helpful for building others up according to their needs, that it may benefit those who listen.*"

For the record, I'm far from having this under control. However, reading, studying, and memorizing this verse will help you to stop and think.

Psalm 119:11 addresses this tendency: "*I have hidden your word in my heart that I might not sin against you.*" Please note the word "might." This is not a guarantee. You have to devote yourself to a life of not only studying but living the Word of God.

Here are three applications:

1. Do not talk about other people.
2. Do not listen or participate in gossip or slander about other people.
3. Do no wrong or sin against others.

Psalm 15:4 says, *"...who despises a vile person but honors those who fear the Lord; who keeps an oath even when it hurts, and does not change their mind."*

Observation. While studying, the translation I use most often is the New International Version. However, as a reference, I use many different translations. Although they are each different, the similarities are quite incredible. For instance, when I want to read the Bible at length, I choose The Message, authored by Eugene Peterson. If I have trouble understanding a verse, Peterson's version, which is written in contemporary language, can be immensely helpful.

When I saw the first part of this verse and noticed the word "vile," I decided to dig deeper to understand it better. What kind of person would God want me to despise?

I looked up the verse in several translations. The Message used the word "despicable"; the New American Bible (Revised Edition), "wicked"; the New Living Translation, "flagrant sinner"; and the New American Standard Bible, "reprobate." *The Students Bible Dictionary* defines vile as "despised, filthy, dishonoured."[53] *Collins English Dictionary* really hammers this home: "abominably wicked, shameful or evil, morally despicable, tending to humiliate or degrade."[54]

Psalm 12:7–8 says, *"You, Lord, will keep the needy safe and will protect us forever from the wicked, who freely strut about when what is vile is honored by the human race."*

No matter how you define this word, no matter how many different translations you look up, one thing is clear: this is not a good individual.

Now, I want to admire people who fear the Lord. That has value. It's difficult to explain why someone would want to be grouped in with celebrities, but it happens all the time. I have no issue with people who are very wealthy. As a matter of fact, even some multimillionaires or billionaires don't have enough money, because they use their wealth to further the kingdom and help many in need. You regularly hear stories of very wealthy people building churches in faraway lands, supporting the hungry, and sponsoring missionaries. These people deserve everything they have and more. It is not money that is the root of all evil; it is the love of money.

John MacArthur writes of three positive phased ethical characteristics:

1. He views the reprobate as rejected.
2. He respects the people of God.
3. He holds himself accountable.[55]

Warren Wiersbe said, "People with integrity will honour others who have integrity and who fear the Lord. They will not be deceived by the flatterers or enticed by the sinful."[56]

Psalm 119:63 says, *"I am a friend to all who fear you, to all who follow your precepts."* Psalm 1:1 asserts, *"Blessed is the one who does not walk in step with the wicked or stand in the way that sinners take or sit in the company of mockers."*

William MacDonald wrote,

> Moral distinctions are not blurred in their vision. They discern between sin and righteousness, darkness and light, evil and good. He despises a vile man in the sense that he outspokenly witnesses against the ungodliness. On the other hand, he identifies himself in open approval with everyone in the household of faith. Once he has made a promise, he stands by it, even if it results in financial loss.[57]

Your word is your bond and a handshake is a handshake. This was also true in the Old Testament, when people would give oaths. In the New Testament, Jesus gives us a new message: *"All you need to say is simply 'Yes' or 'No'; anything beyond this comes from the evil one"* (Matthew 5:37). Further, James 5:12 says, *"Above all, my brothers and sisters, do not swear— not by heaven or by earth or by anything else. All you need to say is a simple "Yes" or "No." Otherwise you will be condemned."* Charles Ryrie wrote,

In the Old Testament the emphasis on the sanctity of oaths led to the feeling that ordinary phrasing need not be truthful or binding. Jesus, however, taught (Matthew 5:37) that we should say and mean yes or no and never equivocate.[58]

Application. There are four areas of application for this verse:

1. Do not fellowship with groups of people involved in immoral activities.
2. Speak out against wrong.
3. Honour your fellow Christians as brothers and sisters in Christ.
4. Stand by what you say, no matter the outcome.

Psalm 15:5 says, *"…who lends money to the poor without interest; who does not accept a bribe against the innocent. Whoever does these things will never be shaken."*

Observation. As we move into the final verse of this incredible psalm, David moves to some financial issues. This verse isn't saying that it's wrong to charge interest to someone for a loan; it instructs us not to charge excessive interest. There's a term for a person who participates in this type of transaction: a loan shark.

As a rule, I will never loan money to anyone, including family members. I have no issue giving money to someone who's in need, but loans carry a lot of baggage. I'm not a financial expert, but if a financial institute declines a loan to someone, there must be a reason, and who am I to question this? Also, loaning money to someone you know can cause tension if payments are missed or if they decide not to repay the money.

Exodus 22:25 says, *"If you lend money to one of my people among you who is needy, do not treat it like a business deal; charge no interest."* The Old Testament Law says that an Israelite wasn't to charge a fellow Israelite any interest. If this is the way it was under the Law, should we not do the same as Christians under grace? The verse is stating that you shouldn't take advantage of someone in dire financial straits. When you take advantage, you will surely reap what you sow.

Psalm 15

A common phrase used today says, "Everyone has their price." Unfortunately, this is often true in today's society, just as it was back in Old Testament times. This pertains to so many areas of our lives, such as when we pay cash to avoid taxes, give gifts to someone to close a deal, turn a blind eye against an injustice, or pay someone to discredit or bring harm to someone else. It becomes even worse when these things are done against innocent people.

The person of Psalm 15 would never participate in this practice for any reason. William MacDonald said, "Finally, the righteous man does not take a bribe against the innocent. He hates the perversion of justice and disproves the old saying that 'everyone has his price.'"[59]

This then is the type of person who lives for God for eternity. Come to think of it, no one else would be comfortable in God's presence!

John MacArthur lists three negatively cast ethical characteristics:

1. He is not fickle.
2. He is not greedy.
3. He cannot be bought.[60]

Finally, at the conclusion of Psalm 15, God reveals a great promise to His people: "*Whoever does these things will never be shaken*" (Psalm 15:5). A parallel can be found when Jesus was summing up the Sermon on the Mount: "*Therefore everyone who hears these words of mine and puts them into practice is like a wise man who built his house on the rock*" (Matthew 7:24).

This reminds me again of the chorus that says, "On Christ the solid rock I stand, all other ground is sinking sand."[61]

Psalm 112:6–7 tells us, "*Surely the righteous will never be shaken; they will be remembered forever. They will have no fear of bad news; their hearts are steadfast, trusting in the Lord.*"

The New Testament also has some great verses on this topic, including:

David said about him: "'I saw the Lord always before me. Because he is at my right hand, I will not be shaken.'"

—Acts 2:25

Therefore, since we are receiving a kingdom that cannot be shaken, let us be thankful, and so worship God acceptably with reverence and awe…

—Hebrews 12:28

Therefore, my brothers and sisters, make every effort to confirm your calling and election. For if you do these things, you will never stumble, and you will receive a rich welcome into the eternal kingdom of our Lord and Savior Jesus Christ.

—2 Peter 1:10–11

This is a psalm you can use for your entire life as a benchmark or goal to achieve. It is for those who want to be around God and be part of His family. You can in fact take each section and use it to develop a closer walk with the Lord. It is also a psalm to memorize, as it will elevate you in many areas of your life, causing you to rise above any situation and ascend to a higher ground meant for God's people. You can use this psalm as one of accountability to God, showing others that living a righteous life is more important than anything else.

Praise God for providing us with such a directional chapter for life!

Application. There are three main takeaways we can draw from this last verse in the psalm:

1. Never take advantage of people in need.
2. Never take or give a bribe.
3. With God's help, become a Psalm 15 person!

- Chapter Seven -

The Full Armour of God

Now that you identified some foundational attributes for living a life that will not be shaken, it's time to move on to the next challenge you will face as a Christian.

I again met with the apostle Paul and asked him what to do when opposition comes. First, he told me that adversity and hardship will certainly come. As we reviewed his credentials again, I felt confident that he would know how to keep things under control.

"We will never be totally free from sin," Paul said. He wrote in Romans 7:15, *"I do not understand what I do. For want I want to do I do not do, but what I hate I do."* He then explained that we will be caught up in spiritual warfare from the day we receive Jesus onward, and only He can win that battle.

Nonetheless, there is a way to defend ourselves, with God's help. We find this help in the full armour of God. I wanted to know everything about this armour and how God would fight this battle.

Paul went on to explain that as you walk with the Lord, there will always be opposition—and the stronger your faith, the stronger the opposition. Satan doesn't want you to succeed.

You can never lose your salvation once you have truly received Jesus Christ as your Lord and Saviour, but you will struggle. Lies, doubt, and guilt are strong tools of the devil which he will use to try discouraging you and slowing down your growth as a Christian. This is the sin that creeps into our lives. We must listen to the whisper of the Holy Spirit to be aware of what is happening and run from it.

The incredible part is that we have already been forgiven of these very sins! 1 John 1:9 explains, *"If we confess our sins, he is faithful and just and will forgive us our sins and purify us from all unrighteousness."*

While the Holy Spirit is convicting us on the one hand, the devil fights back with lies that manifest in the questions we ask ourselves. For example, "How can you call yourself a Christian when you just lost your temper?" or "Do you honestly think God will mind if you just talk with that woman?"

God wants you to be happy. Always remember that Satan is the father of lies, and he and the fallen angels hate the Lord Jesus, and thus they also hate us, His beloved creation.

I once heard someone explain that living the Christian life is like walking down a street with buildings on both sides, and at the end of the street, Jesus waits for us in all His glory. Nothing could stop me from eventually getting to Jesus. However, as I walk, a window on one of the buildings opens and the devil appears there to tempt me. I stop and look. The longer I look, the stronger his hold becomes. Although I want to get to Jesus, the devil's distractions slow my walk with the Lord.

Always remember that the longer you look at the temptation, the more it will grow. Satan is the master of this, and the earth is his kingdom. You will live with this struggle for the rest of your life, which is why you'll require the full armour of God.

Ephesians 6:10–18 lays out the different pieces of armour:

> *Finally, be strong in the Lord and in his mighty power. Put on the full armor of God, so that you can take your stand against the devil's schemes. For our struggle is not against flesh and blood, but against the rulers, against the authorities, against the powers of this dark world and against the spiritual forces of evil in the heavenly realms. Therefore put on the full armor of God, so that when the day of evil comes, you may be able to stand your ground, and after you have done everything, to stand. Stand firm then, with the belt of truth buckled around your waist, with the breastplate of righteousness in place, and with your feet fitted with the readiness that comes from the gospel of peace. In addition to all this, take up the shield of*

The Full Armour of God

faith, with which you can extinguish all the flaming arrows of the evil one. Take the helmet of salvation and the sword of the Spirit, which is the word of God.

And pray in the Spirit on all occasions with all kinds of prayers and requests. With this in mind, be alert and always keep on praying for all the Lord's people.

Background. Paul said that he wrote the book of Ephesians while in prison, but many scholars have determined that it was not written to the people of Ephesus. Rather, it was meant more as a general letter to all churches.

Immediately I'm struck by how incredible it is that while he was in prison, he wrote many of the letters that went on to change Christianity. I cannot imagine sitting in a prison cell and writing some of the most incredible portions of Scripture ever read. God used Paul in such a mighty way.

"The church of Ephesus was started by my friends Pricilla and Aquilla," Paul said to me. "And later I helped it to become firmly established, pastoring for a while as things settled down."

Acts 19:32 says, *"The assembly was in confusion: Some were shouting one thing, some another. Most of the people did not even know why they were there."* Paul got things back on track and eventually turned the church over to Timothy.

The major issue they faced was that of false teaching, which is a game-changer in any church. Rightly dividing the Word of truth is the answer. When any church moves away from God's Word, you can be sure there will be spiritual battles.

John MacArthur wrote,

> Despite, and partly even because of, a Christian's great blessings in Jesus Christ, he is sure to be tempted by Satan to self-satisfaction and complacency. It is for that reason that, in the last chapter of Ephesians, Paul reminds believers of the full and sufficient armour supplied to them through God's word and by his Spirit and of their need for vigilant and persistent prayer.[62]

Just look at the key words in this strong passage of protection: truth, righteousness, peace, faith, salvation, Word of God, and prayer. In this chapter, we will dive deep into each word and phrase of this passage, all the while preparing for the combat we cannot lose with the Lord in control.

So let us arm ourselves for battle and use the plan God has laid out for us in the book of Ephesians.

Ephesians 6:10 says, *"Finally, be strong in the Lord and in his mighty power."*

Observation. The word "finally" forms the beginning of this verse. This section brings the letter to the Ephesians to a conclusion, and again let me state that this is believed to be a letter to all churches. I think this verse truly sets the tone of the entire subject of the armour of God: we are and never will be a match for Satan.

When you consider the apostle Peter—one of Jesus's inner circle who spent years at His side witnessing miracles and sitting at His feet—you would think that if anyone would be a match for Satan, it would be him. Peter was a tough fisherman who drew his sword against an entire army to stand up for Jesus. In Luke 22:31, Jesus said, *"Simon, Simon, Satan has asked to sift all of you as wheat."*

Nowhere in Scripture does it state we stand any chance on our own against the attacks of Satan. I've heard people say they can challenge Satan, and I have to tell you, I want no part of that. If he could take out Peter, he could certainly take me out.

Our base and foundation has to be the Lord Jesus. A great hymn written by Martin Luther says,

> And though this world, with devils filled,
> should threaten to undo us,
> we will not fear, for God has willed
> his truth to triumph through us.
> The prince of darkness grim,
> we tremble not for him;
> his rage we can endure,
> for lo! his doom is sure;
> one little word shall fell him.[63]

This is not our battle. The following scriptures affirm:

Wait for the Lord; be strong and take heart and wait for the Lord.
—Psalm 27:14

"Be strong, all you people of the land," declares the Lord, "and work. For I am with you," declares the Lord Almighty.
—Haggai 2:4

Yet he did not waver through unbelief regarding the promise of God, but was strengthened in his faith and gave glory to God…
—Romans 4:20

Be on your guard; stand firm in the faith; be courageous; be strong.
—1 Corinthians 16:13

…and his incomparably great power for us who believe. That power is the same as the mighty strength…
—Ephesians 1:19

You then, my son, be strong in the grace that is in Christ Jesus.
—2 Timothy 2:1

Application. From this passage, I have identified three applications:

1. Lean on the mighty power of God being led by the promptings of the Holy Spirit.
2. Continually study God's Word to be battle-ready.
3. Remember that our hope and strength comes from the Lord Jesus.

Ephesians 6:11 says, *"Put on the full armor of God, so that you can take your stand against the devil's schemes."*

Observation. Paul explained that those who prepare for battle must have the proper equipment, and the believer has to step up and put the armour on. You can't participate in spiritual warfare without the tools God will provide. Without this armour, you'll be defenceless. Certainly, God will fight for you, but it is our responsibility to be ready. This armour is of the divine nature and you need it all. A few pieces just will not cut it. Whatever you do in your life, you must be prepared.

In the world of business, one doesn't make a major presentation without doing research and understanding the needs of those in attendance. You need to know in detail, moment by moment, what you are going to do and say. In our lives, we wouldn't go into personal or business meetings without putting on the armour of preparation. How much more should we prepare to know the will of God and apply it to our lives? If God is providing armour, not only should we put it on, but we should know every part of it intimately and understand why we need to wear it.

Romans 13:12 says, *"The night is nearly over; the day is almost here. So let us put aside the deeds of darkness and put on the armor of light."* 2 Corinthians 10:4 says, *"The weapons we fight with are not the weapons of the world. On the contrary, they have divine power to demolish strongholds."*

The devil's schemes can seem ominous. Paul explained that we can be sure he will plan things against God's people. You can be certain the devil knows when and where to attack us at our weakest moment and weakest points. He will fire shots of recent moral failures, discouragement, confusion, lack of faith, or anything else that will take us off-course. He is the master of deception and lies.

We know he has no power to take away our salvation, but he will do everything to distract us—and his timing is impeccable. If he cannot take us out one way, he'll try other tactics to extinguish our flame and passion to follow Jesus.

The dictionary defines a scheme as "a systematic plan for a course of action."[64] This is a perfect definition of what Satan attempts to do in our lives. Pay attention to this. If something feels wrong, run from it and seek the guidance of the Holy Spirit and God's Word to stay on track. The Word will never mislead you in your walk with the Lord Jesus.

Application. There are three applications to take from this passage:

1. Run from any and all evil that comes across your path.
2. Seek first God's Word and pray.
3. Trust in the Lord with all your heart, and lean not on your own understanding (Proverbs 3:5).

Ephesians 6:12 says, *"For our struggle is not against flesh and blood, but against the rulers, against the authorities, against the powers of this dark world and against the spiritual forces of evil in the heavenly realms."*

Observation. Paul initially makes it clear that we will struggle. He does not wonder *if* we will struggle, but rather assumes that we will. Thus, struggle is inevitable when you're a believer in Jesus Christ, especially if you're living a life that brings honour and glory to Him.

The struggles we face here are not based on our day-to-day activities and interactions with others; they come from a much darker place that involves unseen demonic forces attempting to steer us away from the Lord. They are very clever and seemingly come out of nowhere.

John MacArthur explains,

> Struggle or wrestle are terms used in hand-to-hand combat. Struggling or wrestling features trickery and deception, like Satan and his hosts when they attack. Coping with deceptive temptation requires, truth and righteousness. The four designations describe the different strata and ranking of those demons and the evil supernatural empire in which they operate. Satan's forces of darkness are highly structured for the most destructive purposes.[65]

It appears we are in a battle we cannot win—but be of good cheer! There is good news. William MacDonald comments,

> While it is true that they cannot indwell a true believer, they can oppress and harass them. The Christian should not be morbidly occupied with the subject of demonism; neither should he live in fear of demons. In the armour of God, he has all he needs to hold his ground against their onslaughts.[66]

Application. Here are three takeaways we can draw from this verse:

1. Be aware of this struggle, but don't let it consume you.
2. Fully understand and put on the armour of God.
3. If something seems out of sorts, seek God.

Ephesians 6:13 says, *"Therefore put on the full armor of God, so that when the day of evil comes, you may be able to stand your ground, and after you have done everything, to stand."*

Observation. Paul explained that this verse instructs us to get battle-ready. Note again that it's not *if* the evil is coming, but *when*. We live in a very evil and sin-filled world that is ruled by Satan and the powers of this world. When you put your hope and trust in the world, you're putting your hope and trust in Satan.

The majority of people believe totally in this world's system, which is understandable, as they don't know Jesus as their Lord and Saviour. In this present age, they desire instant rewards. They're headed in an awfully bad direction.

Most Christians understand that the world and its desires will pass away, as John wrote, but what I don't understand is why so many Christians still put way too much faith in this world.

This verse also talks about standing your ground, which to me is an important part of our Christian lives. What do we stand for? What are our moral absolutes? When I thought about the things I stood for and fought for before becoming a Christian and the things I stand for today as a Christian, I noticed that the two lists were completely different.

It has been said, "Right is right, even if everyone is against it, and wrong is wrong, even if everyone is for it."[67]

Deep down, I truly feel that most people know right from wrong. However, today a new term has crept in: "situational ethics." This term gives people licence to see and interpret things any way they want.

Earlier on, we looked at two teachers, one being false. Today, people make up their own set of ethics, morals, and laws—and we must stay far away from this type of thinking. If something doesn't fit into God's plan, run as far away as you can!

God's Word warned us about this centuries ago! 2 Timothy 4:1–4 says,

> *In the presence of God and of Christ Jesus, who will judge the living and the dead, and in view of his appearing and his kingdom, I give you this charge: Preach the word; be prepared in season and out of season; correct, rebuke and encourage—with great patience and careful instruction. For the time will come when people will not put up with sound doctrine. Instead, to suit their own desires, they will gather around them a great number of teachers to say what their itching ears want to hear. They will turn their ears away from the truth and turn aside to myths.*

We are seeing this play out before our eyes. If you decide you're going to stand for the Christian life, you had better know what you stand for and make sure it's based on God's Word. Always remember what 1 John 2:17 teaches: "*The world and its desires pass away, but whoever does the will of God lives forever.*" Also note that 2 Timothy 4:2 states, "*Preach the word; be prepared in season and out of season; correct, rebuke and encourage—with great patience and careful instruction.*"

Once you know what you stand for, the next step in this battle is to arm yourself with the weapons of spiritual warfare. This is very exciting, and my prayer is that you will burn this into your minds as you prepare to live the life God has planned for you.

Application. Here are three ways in which we can apply this to our lives:

1. Have a crystal-clear idea of what you stand for.
2. Make sure your stance is based on God's Word.
3. Do your best to correct, rebuke, and encourage others, with great patience and careful instruction.

Next, we're going to move on to the weapons of spiritual warfare God has supplied for all of His children.

Even as I write this, I cannot believe that I am a child of the King, the Most High God! We are part of the family of the Lord. The Bible puts it so well in 1 Peter 2:9: *"But you are a chosen people, a royal priesthood, a holy nation, God's special possession, that you may declare the praises of him who called you out of darkness into his wonderful light."*

We also read in Romans 8:15–17,

> *The Spirit you received does not make you slaves, so that you live in fear again; rather, the Spirit you received brought about your adoption to sonship. And by him we cry, "Abba, Father." The Spirit himself testifies with our spirit that we are God's children. Now if we are children, then we are heirs—heirs of God and co-heirs with Christ, if indeed we share in his sufferings in order that we may also share in his glory.*

There it is again—we will suffer if we take a stand for Jesus, but we will also share in His glory. What an incredible promise!

A soldier is trained in warfare. We as Christians are trained in spiritual warfare, and we must train for all-out war. These seven weapons will require a lifetime of consistent training to hone, and they'll only be effective with God's help. Surely if we try this on our own, we will fail. May God help us to train and use these weapons, and then teach our families to do the same.

Let us take a look at each individual piece of armour from God's point of view and learn how to use it to live a victorious Christian life.

First up is the belt of truth. Ephesians 6:14 says, *"Stand firm then, with the belt of truth buckled around your waist, with the breastplate of righteousness in place…"*

Observation. Paul took the time to describe the belt worn by Roman soldiers in his day. It wrapped around their waists and had strands of leather hanging in front to protect their loins. This belt also held weapons of war, such as swords and daggers. The belt or girdle held everything together as the tunic was a loose-fitting cloth, and this could pose a problem in hand-to-hand combat.

The definition of truth is as follows: "genuine, honest, sincere, actual, reliable, able to be trusted. Actual fact rather than pretense, appearance or charm."[68] Our armour gives us our integrity, and in the same way that belt held together the garments of Roman soldiers, truth holds our lives together and is an essential part of Christian living.

Telling the truth requires deliberate action. Psalm 15:2 discusses the one *"who speaks the truth from their heart."* Understanding the truth of God's Word requires practice and study, or it won't work. Satan is a liar, and if we participate in those lies our lives will fall apart and we will be destroyed. The truth will defeat him, however.

Test everything against the Word of God and your strength will be renewed. Isaiah 40:31 reveals that *"those who hope in the Lord will renew their strength. They will soar on wings like eagles; they will run and not grow weary; they will walk and not be faint."*

When you have a clear conscience and live with integrity, you can face the enemy without fear. Truth will defeat those who come after you.

Jesus tells us that truth frees us, as He says in John 8:31–32: *"If you hold to my teaching, you are really my disciples. Then you will know the truth, and the truth will set you free."* God is the source of truth, and Jesus is called the truth: *"I am the way and the truth and the life. No one comes to the Father except through me"* (John 14:6).

The Old Testament speaks of God as truth and the New Testament speaks of Jesus as truth. We must be obedient, loyal, and consistent to the truth, without any trace of falsehood, insincerity, or unfaithfulness. Would people rate you as being truthful and a person of integrity?

Application. Here are two ways you can apply this verse:

1. Tell the truth and be free, which demands a deliberate action.
2. Know the truth by studying and applying the Word of God to your life.

Next up: the breastplate of righteousness.

Observation. The breastplate was a protective garment made of metal, woven chain, or leather, and it was worn by the soldier on the upper part of his body to protect the vital organs.

Paul explained that this piece of armour is quite significant, as it covers the heart. The heart is not only the most important part of our body, but also the part of ourselves that God knows better than we do. As 1 Samuel 16:7 says, *"People look at the outward appearance, but the Lord looks at the heart."* This demonstrates the contrast between the divine and human perspectives. Righteousness practiced by Christians is a way to protect your heart from Satan. When you do what is right in God's eyes, you cannot go wrong.

One of my favourite verses in Scripture is Matthew 5:6, which says, *"Blessed are those who hunger and thirst for righteousness, for they will be filled."* Now that's what I'm talking about! This is why I love to study this incredible book. When you get into it and dig and hunt for treasure, you will be filled—it is a promise.

Righteousness means being honest, good, humble, and fair to others. It means standing up for weaker people. Debbie McDaniel, in an article regarding the armour of God, said most poignantly,

> The enemy wants to attack you not only with lies, but also with impurity. He wants you to read filthy magazines, watch immoral movies, and engage in all temptations of the flesh. The bottom line is that Satan wants to get into your heart and mind. He's looking for a crack in the armour. And don't be fooled. Satan knows where that crack is. Is your heart pure before God? If not, you cannot win the battle.[69]

There is an incredible description in 1 Peter 5:8, which advises, *"Be alert and of sober mind. Your enemy the devil prowls around like a roaring lion looking for someone to devour."* That should make you sit up and take notice. Comprehend what the scripture is saying—the devil is just waiting to pounce. Satan wants to completely destroy your entire testimony.

2 Corinthians 5:21 says, *"God made him [Jesus] who had no sin to be sin for us, so that in him we might become the righteousness of God."* Charles Ryrie, in his commentary on this verse, says, "Here is the heart of the gospel: The sinless Saviour has taken our sins that we might have God's

righteousness."[70] Simply put, a righteous person is one who, among other things, does what is right.

As stated earlier, right is right even if everyone says it is wrong, and wrong is wrong even if everyone says it is right. 1 Thessalonians 5:8 says, *"But since we belong to the day, let us be sober, putting on faith and love as a breastplate…"* Honestly, I feel that most people do know and understand right from wrong but make specific choices to do wrong. This is sin.

Application. I've identified three areas of application for this verse:

1. In all your actions, remember that God sees your heart.
2. Do what is right and stay clear of wrongdoing.
3. Hunger and thirst for righteousness and be prepared for God to fill and protect you.

Now let's talk about the gospel of peace. Ephesians 6:15 says, *"…and with your feet fitted with the readiness that comes from the gospel of peace."*

Observation. Paul wanted to discuss the type of life we should live as Christians. The gospel is a term that means "good news." Isaiah 52:7 says, *"How beautiful on the mountains are the feet of those who bring good news, who proclaim peace, who bring good tidings, who proclaim salvation, who say to Zion, 'Your God reigns!'"* Wow! What a verse. This is the type of person I long to be one day. Romans 10:15 says, *"As it is written: 'How beautiful are the feet of those who bring good news!'"*

Even in times of war, Paul talks about peace. It almost sounds oxymoronic to discuss war and peace at the same time. But as we move forward in our preparation for battle, peace must be one of our weapons.

When people describe you, would the word "peacemaker" make the cut? When conflicts brew around you, do you join in or try to bring peace? Peace, in Hebrew, is *shalom*. This was used often as a greeting. Peace is something most people dream of having, and it is possible.

Over the years, many people have asked me to pray for peace in their lives—peace for major decisions such as family issues, finances, the choice of marriage partner, career moves, disputes, church problems, etc. This is a true gift if you can find it.

The peace that comes from the world and its desires is completely different than the peace that comes from God. Online, I found a good definition of God's peace:

> According to the Bible, the peace of God, "which transcends all understanding," is the harmony and calmness of body, mind, and spirit that supersedes earthly circumstances. Nearly all of the letters of Paul start with the phrase "Grace and peace to you from God our Father and the Lord Jesus Christ." Throughout scripture, we find that peace is defined as a blessing from God and harmonious with His character…
>
> If God is inherently peaceful, then to appreciate God is to live in His peace. The nearer we move to Him, the more of His peace we can experience. Thankfully, the Bible provides us specific guidance about how to be closer to Him.[71]

Philippians 4:7 says, *"And the peace of God, which transcends all understanding, will guard your hearts and your minds in Christ Jesus."* When we grow in our knowledge of the wisdom and prosperity of God's love for us, our minds and spirits develop a peaceful faith in His power and grace. We begin to recognize that He really will make all things work together for our good and that His purposes will be achieved.

Colossians 3:15 says, *"Let the peace of Christ rule in your hearts, since as members of one body you were called to peace. And be thankful."* The last word in this verse is key to Christian living: we must be thankful. We have so much to thank God for, starting with salvation, forgiveness of sin, and the fact that our names are written in heaven. Be a thankful person!

Let me conclude this observation with a great promise from the Beatitudes, which form the beginning of the Sermon on the Mount. How would you like to have the distinction of being called sons of God? Well, Jesus said in Matthew 5:9, *"Blessed are the peacemakers, for they will be called children of God."*

So, as you can see, peace plays an enormous part not only in our battles, but in our lives.

Application. Here are three ways you can apply this verse in your life:

1. Be a peacemaker, with God's help.
2. Spread the good news of Jesus.
3. Be a thankful person.

Next up we'll discuss the shield of faith. Ephesians 6:16 says, *"In addition to all this, take up the shield of faith, with which you can extinguish all the flaming arrows of the evil one."*

Observation. The Roman shield was approximately two feet by four feet. It was mostly made of wood, with a few layers glued together to form its curved shape. Some extra strips of wood were glued to the back to strengthen it. The shield was then covered in leather and a sheet of linen cloth. Designs were usually painted onto the front.

In battle, the shield was held with the arm straight, gripping it in the middle where a hole was cut. This hole was protected by a metal boss, a hemisphere of iron with an iron plate around it. The soldier could push this boss into his enemy to knock him off-balance. Sheepskin was used above the handle to make the grip more comfortable. The rim was protected either with strips of bronze or with leather.

There are many references to faith and faithfulness in the Bible, and it would be a good exercise to look up the word in a concordance and review as many references as you can find. You will quickly find that faith is an important part of our journey through God's Word. World's One Bible dictionary defines faith as such:

> In the original language of the New Testament, the noun "faith" and the verb "believe" are different parts of the same word. Although faith involves belief, by far the most important characteristic of faith (in the Biblical sense) is reliance or trust.[72]

As Christians, we fully understand that we are saved by faith, as stated in Ephesians 2:8–9. That's not what we're talking about here in the sense of armour. Christians are not only saved by faith; they live by faith. We continue to rely on the promise and power of the unseen God rather than on what we see and experience in the visible world.

Hebrews 11:1 explains, "*Now faith is confidence in what we hope for and assurance about what we do not see.*" In the next chapter of Hebrews, faith is reinforced: "*[Let us fix] our eyes on Jesus, the pioneer and perfecter of faith*" (Hebrews 12:2).

It takes faith to believe in God, as we do not see Him. However, when you look around and see His creation, it doesn't take much faith to believe that someone has put all this together. Where did everything come from? Romans 1:20 says, "*For since the creation of the world God's invisible qualities—his eternal power and divine nature—have been clearly seen, being understood from what has been made, so that people are without excuse.*"

Faith produces sincere obedience in our lives. This will become a part of our everyday living, trusting in Jesus to guide our lives, especially through the fiery trials that come our way. Romans 1:17 says, "*For in the gospel the righteousness of God is revealed—a righteousness that is by faith from first to last, just as it is written: 'The righteous will live by faith.'*"

Romans is a great book regarding faith, and it gives you an example of where to find faith: "*Consequently, faith comes from hearing the message, and the message is heard through the word about Christ*" (Romans 10:17). There is more to faith than just believing; we have to do something.

Again, it is important to remember that Paul is talking to Christians here, as what I'm about to share is not focused on earning your salvation—that can only come by asking God to forgive your sins, having a heart of repentance, and accepting the gift of salvation through Jesus Christ our Lord. Once we have this life in Christ, a difference must become evident in us, whereby we bear fruit by doing good and caring for others.

After you have received Jesus, Ephesians 2:10 states, "*For we are God's handiwork, created in Christ Jesus to do good works, which God prepared in advance for us to do.*" Faith on its own is not the faith Paul is talking about in this passage.

James, the half-brother of Jesus, makes some direct comments regarding this and gives a stern warning about those who believe and don't follow it up with some type of good deeds:

> *What good is it, my brothers and sisters, if someone claims to have faith but has no deeds? Can such faith save them? Suppose a brother*

or a sister is without clothes and daily food. If one of you says to them, "Go in peace; keep warm and well fed," but does nothing about their physical needs, what good is it? In the same way, faith by itself, if it is not accompanied by action, is dead.
But someone will say, "You have faith; I have deeds."
Show me your faith without deeds, and I will show you my faith by my deeds. You believe that there is one God. Good! Even the demons believe that—and shudder.

—James 2:14–19

As is made clear in this passage, you can see there is more to faith than just believing.

When the flaming arrows of the evil one come upon you, your faith will come into action and your shield will become a defensive weapon.

On our own, we are no match for Satan in this world without faith. Only through faith in God can we overcome the world. 1 John 5:5 says, *"Who is it that overcomes the world? Only the one who believes that Jesus is the Son of God."* As you grow in your faith, you can be assured that Satan will come after you. 1 Peter 5:8 asserts, *"Be alert and of sober mind. Your enemy the devil prowls around like a roaring lion looking for someone to devour."*

You need to prepare for the evil one to send you seeds of worry, doubt, and discouragement. These are his most common flaming arrows. There are times when I pray for personal concerns close to my heart, like family members struggling with their faith or not walking with the Lord, and seeds of doubt can enter my mind. Why is God not answering my prayer? These doubts come directly from the pit of hell. God's will and timing are all that matter. I have great peace when I begin to pray to Jesus with a surrendered life and turn those I love over to His care.

Instead of living in fear, there is hope. Peter tells us in the next three verses that calm assurance can come from God:

Resist him, standing firm in the faith, because you know that the family of believers throughout the world is undergoing the same kind of sufferings.

> *And the God of all grace, who called you to his eternal glory in Christ, after you have suffered a little while, will himself restore you and make you strong, firm and steadfast. To him be the power for ever and ever. Amen.*
>
> —1 Peter 5:9–11

Hebrews 13:5 concludes, *"Never will I leave you; never will I forsake you."* This verse goes way back in the Old Testament, when Moses spoke to the people of Israel in Deuteronomy 31:6: *"Be strong and courageous. Do not be afraid or terrified because of them, for the Lord your God goes with you; he will never leave you nor forsake you."* Now that's power!

Application. Here are three areas where you can apply this verse:

1. Keep your faith strong through study, worship, and prayer.
2. Be prepared for flaming arrows of worry, doubt, and discouragement.
3. Make sure your faith has actions attached to it, such as good deeds and helping others.

Let's move on to discuss the helmet of salvation. Ephesians 6:17 says, *"Take the helmet of salvation and the sword of the Spirit, which is the word of God."*

Observation. In the Roman army, the helmet served as protection for one's head, and it was always a major target in battle. This was a vital piece of the armour, as an attack to the head could result in instant death. More specifically, a helmet complements the skull in protecting the brain.

The word helmet comes from *helm*, a medieval word for protective combat headgear. It was a helmet made of bronze, which in its later styles covered the entire head and neck, with slits for the eyes and mouth. A large curved projection protected the nape of the neck.

In this part of Ephesians, Paul is speaking to Christians, those who have already been saved. Salvation in the here and now is revealed when believers continue to experience the saving power of God in victory over sin in their daily lives.

In the same manner, we need protection from our thoughts and hearts. This occurs by what I see with my own eyes. The world will throw all kinds of garbage my way, and I must guard myself against it. If I stay away from temptation, I will be blessed for doing so.

Psalm 1:1 says, *"Blessed is the one who does not walk in step with the wicked or stand in the way that sinners take or sit in the company of mockers…"* The very next verse tells us how to combat this: *"…but whose delight is in the law of the Lord, and who meditates on his law day and night"* (Psalm 1:2).

The key to protecting your mind is by reading and studying the Word of God. John MacArthur wrote,

> Satan seeks to destroy a believer's assurance of salvation with his weapons of doubt and discouragement. This is clear from Paul's reference to the helmet as "the hope of salvation." 1 Thessalonians 5:8c says, "and the hope of salvation as a helmet." But although a Christian's feelings about his salvation may be seriously damaged by Satan-inspired doubt, his salvation itself is eternally protected and he need not fear its loss. Satan wants to curse the believer with doubts, but the Christian can be strong in God's promise of eternal salvation in Scripture. Security is a fact; assurance is a feeling the comes to the obedient Christian.[73]

In his first letter, Peter opens with a great promise about this security we look forward to as we walk with Jesus. As 1 Peter 1:3–9 says,

> *Blessed be the God and Father of our Lord Jesus Christ! According to his great mercy, he has caused us to be born again to a living hope through the resurrection of Jesus Christ from the dead, to an inheritance that is imperishable, undefiled, and unfading, kept in heaven for you, who by God's power are being guarded through faith for a salvation ready to be revealed in the last time. In this you rejoice, though now for a little while, if necessary, you have been grieved by various trials, so that the tested genuineness of your faith—more precious than gold that perishes though it is tested by fire—may be found to result in praise and glory and honor at the revelation of*

Jesus Christ. Though you have not seen him, you love him. Though you do not now see him, you believe in him and rejoice with joy that is inexpressible and filled with glory, obtaining the outcome of your faith, the salvation of your souls. (ESV)

I'm not sure if there's a better description in all of Scripture of our life on earth and what is to follow after receiving Jesus!

The absolute greatest meaning of salvation is the saving grace of Jesus Christ. When you take time to reflect on this, nothing in this world can harm you, for you are saved and your name is written in heaven. No one can take that away from you, not even death.

My life should be totally consumed in living for Jesus Christ, because of my salvation in Him. Through Jesus, I have received eternal life and I must never, ever take this for granted.

Lord, help me thank You every day for Your saving grace and death on the cross.

Let me close with this with an encouragement from Philippians 1:6: *"…being confident of this, that he who began a good work in you will carry it on to completion until the day of Christ Jesus."*

Application. I've identified three applications of this verse for my daily life:

1. Thank God every day for your salvation in Jesus!
2. Protect your mind and heart by studying and meditating on God's Word.
3. Live a life consumed by your walk with the Lord.

Next up is the sword of the Spirit, which is also mentioned in Ephesians 6:17: *"Take the helmet of salvation and the sword of the Spirit, which is the word of God."*

Observation. First, let's examine the Roman sword. The website Reliks.com provides a great description of the Roman sword and its uses:

> The sword carried by the Roman soldier is the Roman Gladius. This short sword combined with expert military tactics has

certainly carved its way into the history books as a fearsome and respected weapon.

The word "Gladius" is believed to have come from the Celtiberians who were a Celtic speaking people from Hispania (The Iberian Peninsula). The Celts there carried a very similar sword that was known as the Gladius Hispaniensis. The Roman legions began carrying a sword of this similar design a couple [hundred] years BC. After the conquest of Hispania. A derivative directly from the Gladius sword was the Gladiator. The gladiator would be the swordsman who carried the gladius. Another derivative, strangely enough, of the gladius is the Gladiolus or the "little sword"...

The Roman Gladius was most effectively used in formation behind the protection of a Roman shield wall. The soldiers would interlock their shields (scutum) giving their opponents virtually no target to strike. They would thrust beside or over the shields cutting down their enemies while the formation advanced...

The Roman Gladius was known for its powerful thrust, but they also held an exceptional edge and were also used for slashing and cutting.[74]

Now let's look at the sword of the Spirit, which is the Word of God. Of all the seven pieces of armour mentioned in Ephesians 6, the sword is the only offensive weapon; the other six are intended for defence.

You think the Roman sword was sharp and effective? The Bible also provides a great definition of the sword in Hebrews 4:12–13:

For the word of God is alive and active. Sharper than any double-edged sword, it penetrates even to dividing soul and spirit, joints and marrow; it judges the thoughts and attitudes of the heart. Nothing in all creation is hidden from God's sight. Everything is uncovered and laid bare before the eyes of him to whom we must give account.

This is why I love God's Word! Can you imagine an instrument that you use daily that gives you such a straight and narrow perspective on any topic you choose? I've often experienced the stab of conviction in my own life when I strayed from the will of God.

When you're faced with any issue in life—and let me say it again, *any*—the Word of God will give you direction. When the Holy Spirit convicts you of some type of wrongdoing, you have two choices. The first choice is to continue on with the transgression or smear against God. The second choice is to take the time to look up the error of your way in the Bible and make the changes in your life and apply what you have learned, thus glorifying God. It's just that simple!

It's not that we don't know the answer, it's just that we don't want to change the lifestyle we're living. There is no question that sin can be pleasurable for a short time, but it will come back and attack you and have long-term effects on your mind and heart, effects that will take years to recover from.

The answer is to listen to the prodding of the Holy Spirit and act on it by spending time in God's Word. The entire reason I wrote this book is to direct people to the greatest book ever written, which has the power to change their lives. Over the years, I've used the Bible as a reference point in many discussions. When you're backed up by God's Word, you can't go wrong.

The following are verses of reference for the Word of God which form a good basis of study.

> *Blessed rather are those who hear the word of God and obey it.*
> —Luke 11:28

> *But the word of God continued to spread and flourish.*
> —Acts 12:24

> *And we also thank God continually because, when you received the word of God, which you heard from us, you accepted it not as a human word, but as it actually is, the word of God, which is indeed at work in you who believe.*
> —1 Thessalonians 2:13

The Bible will change your life the more you use it. I would like to conclude this section with a great verse to encourage you to know and study your Bible:

Do your best to present yourself to God as one approved, a worker who does not need to be ashamed and who correctly handles the word of truth.

—2 Timothy 2:15

John MacArthur accurately explained the sword of the Spirit this way:

As the sword was the soldier's only weapon, so God's word is the only needed weapon, infinitely more powerful than any of Satan's. It was used both defensively to fend off Satan's attacks and offensively to help destroy the enemy's strategies. It is the truth of Scripture.[75]

My authority comes from the Word of God. I guess I would be classified as a chapter-and-verse person. In my life to date, the Bible has been the source of every one of my questions, and it has provided me with very sound answers. It is my comfort and peace, and when I stray or stop listening to God's Word, my life goes downhill.

When steeped in the study of God's Word, I soon learn that life isn't all about me; it's about Jesus. How long will the Bible be effective? Jesus said in Matthew 24:35, *"Heaven and earth will pass away, but my words will never pass away."* You can count on it!

Application. Here are three applications from this discussion of the sword of the Spirit.

1. Always turn to God's Word for direction.
2. Use the sword of the Spirit, accurately backing it up with God's Word.
3. Live a life in full view of God.

Next, we will discuss the weapon of prayer. Ephesians 6:18 says, *"And pray in the Spirit on all occasions with all kinds of prayers and requests. With this in mind, be alert and always keep on praying for all the Lord's people."*

Observation. The *World's Bible Dictionary* defines prayer this way: "Prayer is that activity of believers whereby they communicate with God, worshipping him, praising him, thanking him, confessing to him and making requests to him."[76]

What a privilege it is to be able to come to the feet of the Lord and commune with Him. Some ask, "Why pray when God knows everything?" God created us to be His children and, like any father, He loves to hear from us.

Jesus gives us a guideline from which to pray, and it can be found in the Sermon on the Mount. He begins by telling us not to be hypocritical.

> *And when you pray, do not be like the hypocrites, for they love to pray standing in the synagogues and on the street corners to be seen by others. Truly I tell you, they have received their reward in full. But when you pray, go into your room, close the door and pray to your Father, who is unseen. Then your Father, who sees what is done in secret, will reward you. And when you pray, do not keep on babbling like pagans, for they think they will be heard because of their many words. Do not be like them, for your Father knows what you need before you ask him.*
>
> —Matthew 6:5–8

This is not meant to condemn public prayer; it's meant to question the motive behind the person praying. Believers should set aside certain times when they can be alone with God and pray, as Jesus often did. He also provides a solid agenda to pray:

> *This, then, is how you should pray: "Our Father in heaven, hallowed be your name, your kingdom come, your will be done, on earth as it is in heaven. Give us today our daily bread. And forgive*

us our debts, as we also have forgiven our debtors. And lead us not into temptation, but deliver us from the evil one."

—Matthew 6:9–13

Jesus concludes this section of the sermon with an additional comment on forgiveness: *"For if you forgive other people when they sin against you, your heavenly Father will also forgive you. But if you do not forgive others their sins, your Father will not forgive your sins"* (Matthew 6:14–15). The Lord does not want us to hold grudges and hatred towards others. This is not the DNA of a believer. We are forgiven; therefore, we forgive.

As the years of life go on, and the more I study God's Word and come face to face with His holiness, I can assure you that no one has sinned against me greater than I have sinned against God. If He can forgive me, how can I not forgive others?

There are many ways you can choose to pray, and over the years people have developed different structures to assist in your prayer time.

One such structure is known by the acronym ACTS (adoration, confession, thanksgiving, and supplication), which always put our needs at the end. This is a great strategy, as most people just run through a daily laundry list of things they want God to provide.

Another method involves "praying your hand." Your thumb, being closest to you, means you pray for those closest to you, such as family, friends, neighbours, and co-workers. The first finger, your pointing finger, indicates prayer for those who teach, or whom you learn from, such as pastors, teachers, and mentors. The middle finger is the tallest appendage, and this is where you pray for leaders, politicians, and leaders in your church or work, praying that those in authority may seek God's wisdom and direction. I have been told by piano instructors that the fourth finger is the weakest one, and therefore we then pray for those who are weak or ill, those who have needs. Finally, the baby finger is the smallest, and this is where your personal prayers and needs are communicated. So you pray for the needs of others first and conclude with your needs. It's a good practice to do this on a daily basis.

My prayer time usually takes place in the evening, and during it I pray for different people or situations. I always start my prayer time by singing three hymns from an old hymn book. (Thankfully, no one can hear me.) Then I repeat the Lord's Prayer; it isn't necessary, but it reminds me of what is important and prompts me to start by praising God. When praying for my family, I tell the Lord, "I surrender my life and those I love to Your care."

This is the weekly regiment of my prayers:

- On Monday, I pray for my wife and children.
- On Tuesday, I pray for my grandchildren.
- On Wednesday, I pray for my brothers, nieces, and nephews.
- On Thursday, I pray for the men I have mentored.
- On Friday, I pray the Ten Commandments and Fruits of the Spirit and see how I stack up against them.
- On Saturday, I pray for specific pastors as they prepare for Sunday services.
- Sunday is a day of supplication on which I pray for a collection of things people have asked me to pray about, as well as my personal prayer list.

Prayer time has become the highlight of my day, and I can tell you that once you start a list, it will grow.

Truly, whatever method works for you, just do it. Putting in place a regular routine of daily prayer will change your life in ways you cannot imagine. We live in a very evil world, and some days it appears there is no hope, but once you sit with the Lord and talk to Him, things just seem a lot better. Don't delay. Get started today.

Application. Here are three ways in which you can apply this verse:

1. Pray daily for the needs around you.
2. Ask people, "Can I pray for you and what are your requests?"
3. Become a prayer warrior for Jesus.

Bringing this encouraging section of Scripture to a close, I once came across a prayer by Debbie McDaniel concerning the armour of God. I don't think there is a better way to conclude:

The Full Armour of God

Dear God,

 We thank you that you hold the victory over sin and death in this world. We thank you that you came to set the captives free. We thank you for the redemptive work you've done in our lives. We thank you for freedom and the hope you bring.

 We hold your Word of Truth as a weapon against the enemy's schemes and proclaim he does not have the authority over our lives for we've been set free. Give us wisdom and discernment to recognize his traps and to stand strong against his work. Fill us fresh with the power of your Holy Spirit.

 Today we put on the full armour to guard our lives against attack. We put on the belt of truth to protect against lies and deception. We put on the breastplate of righteousness to protect our hearts from the temptations we battle. We put the gospel of peace on our feet, so we're ready to take your light wherever you send us this day. We choose to walk in the peace and freedom of your Spirit and not be overcome with fear and anxious thoughts. We take up your shield of faith that will extinguish all the darts and threats hurled our way by the enemy. We believe in your power to protect us and choose to trust in you. We put on the helmet of salvation, which covers our minds and thoughts, reminding us we are children of the day, forgiven, set free, saved by the grace of Christ Jesus. We take up the sword of the Spirit, your very Word, the one offensive weapon given to us for battle, which has the power to demolish strongholds, alive, active, and sharper than any double-edged sword.

 We ask for your help in remembering to put on your full armor every day, for you give us all that we need to stand firm in this world. Forgive us God for the times we've been unprepared, too busy to care, or trying to fight and wrestle in our own strength.

 Thank you that we never fight alone, for you are constantly at work on our behalf, shielding, protecting, strengthening, exposing deeds of darkness, bringing to light what needs to be

known, covering us from the cruel attacks we face even when we're unaware. In the powerful name of Jesus,
 Amen.[77]

Part Two

The Journey of Applying God's Word

- Chapter Eight -

Practice What You Preach

The most important part of any Bible study is taking what you've learned and applying it to your life. It makes no sense to acquire all this knowledge of God's Word and then live a completely unrelated life, as if all the knowledge was for naught. You may have heard the saying that says, "Practice what you preach." This is especially pertinent to those who claim to study the Bible.

The Christian life is opposite to the way the world thinks, and when we see a need, we should try to fill that need for the glory of our Lord and Saviour Jesus Christ. The Christian should be constantly looking for ways to serve others and always be ready to help.

Do people know you're a Christian simply because of your words or because of the way you live your life? Sometimes your lifestyle is the only Bible someone will ever read. Let me explain: throughout your journey with Jesus, you may have told someone that you'll pray for them, or mention once that you heard a great message in church. You may feel that they weren't listening or were seemingly uninterested, but most people will take this as a signal and then watch your every move to see if you're the real deal. This doesn't mean you have to lead a perfect life, but it means that if and when you slip in your faith in front of them, you must ask for forgiveness and apologize for your actions.

Now let's meet one of my favourite authors of the Bible. He's the half-brother of the Lord Jesus, and his name is James. James is only Jesus's half-brother because they came from the same mother, but Jesus was born in a very unnatural way—this was known, of course, as the virgin birth.

Background. Experts on the Bible have a lot to say about James, and in this chapter I will share their in-depth commentaries about him. It's important to know the background of this man before we study his portion of Scripture. It has a lot to do with that saying I mentioned, "Practice what you preach."

John MacArthur explains,

> James was the oldest half-brother of Christ and the brother of Jude who also wrote the epistle that bears his name. James at first rejected Jesus as Messiah, but later believed. 1 Corinthians 15:7, "Then he (Jesus) appeared to James (after the resurrection), then to all the apostles." He became a key leader in the Jerusalem church, being called one of the "pillars" of that church, along with Peter and John. Also, known as James the Just because of his devotion to righteousness, he was martyred in AD 62, according to the first century historian Josephus.[78] James wrote with authority of one who had personally seen the resurrected Christ, he was recognized as an associate of the apostles and who was the leader of the Jerusalem church. James can be reliably dated to AD 44–49, making it the earliest written book of the New Testament canon.[79]

Eugene Peterson's introduction to the letter of James says,

> The letter of James shows one of the church's early pastors skillfully going about his work of confronting, diagnosing, and dealing with areas of misbelief and misbehaviour that had turned up in congregations committed to his care. Deep and living wisdom is on display here, wisdom both rare and essential. Wisdom is not primarily knowing the truth, although it certainly includes that; it is a skill in living. For what good is truth if we don't know how to live it? What good is an intention if we can't sustain it?[80]

Chuck Swindoll wrote in his introduction to James,

More than any other book in the New Testament, James places the spotlight on the necessity for believers to act in accordance with our faith. How well do our actions mirror the faith that you proclaim? This is a question that we all struggle to answer well. We would like to point to all the ways our faith and works overlap, but we too often only see gaps and crevices where they do not. As you read the letter from James, focus on the areas he mentions: your actions during trials, your treatment of those less fortunate, the way you speak and relate to others, and the role that money plays in how you live your life. Allow James to encourage you to do good in accordance with the faith you proclaim.[81]

Earlier on in his introduction, Swindoll explains,

Throughout his letter, James contents that real faith produces authentic deeds. In other words, if those who call themselves God's people truly belong to Him, certain deeds, or fruit, will be produced in their lives.[82]

Let's start by taking a look at the complete passage from James that we're going to be talking about in this chapter:

What good is it, my brothers and sisters, if someone claims to have faith but has no deeds? Can such faith save them? Suppose a brother or a sister is without clothes and daily food. If one of you says to them, "Go in peace; keep warm and well fed," but does nothing about their physical needs, what good is it? In the same way, faith by itself, if it is not accompanied by action, is dead.
   But someone will say, "You have faith; I have deeds."
   Show me your faith without deeds, and I will show you my faith by my deeds. You believe that there is one God. Good! Even the demons believe that—and shudder.
—James 2:14–19

Put your seatbelt on as we journey through a very powerful and direct portion of Scripture. The Christian life is about more than just going to church and waiting for the return of Jesus and living in a bubble separated completely from the world. After receiving Jesus, it's time to do the work of the Lord. As the Bible says, the harvest is plentiful, but the labourers are few.

James 2:14 says, *"What good is it, my brothers and sisters, if someone claims to have faith but has no deeds? Can such faith save them?"*

Observation. Normally the question we ask ourselves in this part of the process is "What does it say?" But a better way to observe this passage is by inquiring, "What does it ask?" This is a great question to ask as we start looking into the concept of practicing what you preach.

The verse refers to people who claim to have faith, and therefore this is a message meant for Christians, followers of Jesus Christ. But as John MacArthur explains, "This important phrase governs the interpretation of the entire passage. James does not say this person actually has faith, but that he claims to have it."[83]

I can't emphasize enough the importance of this distinction, and I will continue to say this: it isn't a matter of doing good works to get into heaven. That cannot be done. It is only through repentance and the shed blood of Jesus dying for our sins, along with His forgiveness as we accept Him as Lord and Saviour, that we can get into heaven and escape eternal damnation.

I have to explain the reason I continue to hammer away at this point: when we try to earn our way to heaven through good works, it has nothing to do with God, and everything to do with ourselves. With this mindset, Christianity would become a self-made religion with one's own rules and standards. This would give you control and not God. If that's what you believe, then you won't see the need for a saviour.

I will again point to what Paul says about this in Ephesians 2:8–9: *"For it is by grace you have been saved, through faith—and this is not from yourselves, it is the gift of God—not by works, so that no one can boast."* Chuck Swindoll has a great explanation for this:

> Paul is looking at the root of our salvation (Ephesians 2:8–9), while James is looking at the fruit after salvation. Paul

emphasizes the point that at the time of conversion, the root of salvation is faith alone. James sees that the faith that saves us does not remain alone, though we are saved by faith alone. After salvation, there are things that inevitably happen in our lives that show the reality of salvation.[84]

Another reason I continue to stress this point is for the sake of people who think they're on their way to heaven by their good deeds. Nothing could be further from the truth! This thinking has sent, and will continue to send, many through the gate that leads to destruction. This is a very dangerous game. Please look to the Scriptures for the truth that will set you free.

With that understanding, now is the time to broach this question to Christians: *"What good is it, my brothers and sisters, if someone claims to have faith but has no deeds?"* (James 2:4)

Let's begin with faith. Faith, as described in Hebrews 11:1, is *"confidence in what we hope for and assurance about what we do not see."* The remainder of Hebrews 11, which is also known as the "faith chapter," provides example after example of those who were faithful in the Bible. It's certainly worth reading and studying.

You may recall the story depicted in John 20 where Thomas wouldn't believe that Jesus had been resurrected. As John 20:24–25 tells us,

> *Now Thomas (also known as Didymus), one of the Twelve, was not with the disciples when Jesus came. So the other disciples told him, "We have seen the Lord!"*
>
> *But he said to them, "Unless I see the nail marks in his hands and put my finger where the nails were, and put my hand into his side, I will not believe."*

The story continues a week later when Jesus appeared to Thomas:

> *Then he said to Thomas, "Put your finger here; see my hands. Reach out your hand and put it into my side. Stop doubting and believe."*

> *Thomas said to him, "My Lord and my God!"*
> —John 20:27–28

The story concludes with a great verse on faith that was spoken by Jesus Himself, offering a real encouragement to our faith: *"Because you have seen me, you have believed; blessed are those who have not seen and yet have believed"* (John 20:29). Incredible! Just for believing in Jesus, we are blessed.

That's the kind of faith we as Christians should possess. 2 Corinthians 4:18 says, *"So we fix our eyes not on what is seen, but on what is unseen, since what is seen is temporary, but what is unseen is eternal."*

Charles Ryrie defines faith this way: "Faith gives reality and proof to things unseen, treating them as if they were already objects of sight rather than hope."[85]

Regarding Hebrews 11:1, William MacDonald says,

> This verse is not really a formal definition of faith, rather it is a description of what faith does for us. It makes things hoped for as real as if we already had them, and it provides unshakable evidence that the unseen spiritual blessings of Christianity are absolutely certain and real. In other words, it brings the future within the present and makes the invisible seen.[86]

What a joy it is to have faith in Jesus Christ as Saviour. This in itself should make us thankful for the rest of our lives. We are heaven-bound! James says that it's now time to take this great gift from God and express our thankfulness through deeds.

After Paul states in Ephesians 2:8–9 that we are saved by faith and not by works, the very next verse gives us our marching orders. I've quoted this verse several times already, but this is a good spot to repeat it: *"For we are God's handiwork, created in Christ Jesus to do good works, which God prepared in advance for us to do"* (Ephesians 2:10). God built us to do good deeds and to let our light shine.

Jesus spoke of this concept during the Sermon on the Mount:

> *You are the light of the world. A town built on a hill cannot be hidden. Neither do people light a lamp and put it under a bowl. Instead they put it on its stand, and it gives light to everyone in the house. In the same way, let your light shine before others, that they may see your good deeds and glorify your Father in heaven.*
>
> —Matthew 5:14–16

We as Christians are the light in this very dark world; we should be so overcome with joy that we look for any darkness where we can let our light shine for the glory of the One who saved us! John MacArthur puts this so well: "works or deeds, this refers to all righteous behaviour that conforms to God's revealed word, but specifically, in the context, to acts of compassion."[87]

You don't have to spend years in church, seminary, or Bible study to do good things. You can start immediately! This is what being the light of the world means: when there's a problem, issue, or pain around you, jump in and be a light to whoever is in need.

Christianity is not a spectator sport; we are the players and the Holy Spirit is the coach. You will know when the Spirit leads you to get in the game and turn on your light. If you decide to stay on the sidelines, it's comparable to spending hours creating a presentation to perfection, running through it over and over until you know you'll knock it out of the park, and then deciding not to use it. What good is that?

Believe me, in the course of a day, you'll have many opportunities to do good deeds if you are aware of your surroundings, have a heart of thankfulness toward Jesus, and listen to the promptings of the Holy Spirit.

Now for the "slam dunk" verse: *"If anyone, then, knows the good they ought to do and doesn't do it, it is sin for them"* (James 4:17). Game, set, match!

William MacDonald sums it up this way:

> In this context, to do good is to take God into every aspect of your lives, to live in moment by moment dependence on Him. If we know we should do this, yet fail to do it, we are clearly sinning. Of course, the principle is of broader application. In any area of life, the opportunity to do good makes us responsible to

do it. If we know what is right, we are under obligation to live up to that light. Failure to do so is sin against God, against our neighbour, and against ourselves.[88]

For the record, whenever I've had the opportunity to do good and get in the game, the personal rewards have been fantastic! I don't say this to boast, but to say that it's truly more blessed to give than receive.

Application. Here are three ways to apply this verse to your life:

1. Hang on to your faith through all situations in life.
2. Let your light shine through good deeds done to the glory of Jesus.
3. Get in the game of "doing good"!

James 2:15–16 says, *"Suppose a brother or a sister is without clothes and daily food. If one of you says to them, 'Go in peace; keep warm and well fed,' but does nothing about their physical needs, what good is it?"*

Observation. This is the second great question of the passage. I've found in my life that I often see a need I can fill, and it jumps right out in front of me. You don't have to look very hard to find someone in need. You can't change the world, but you can change things that are right in front of you—especially when you have the means to help out.

Chuck Swindoll tells a marvellous story about going to California to minister. He travelled to Los Angeles to candidate for a large church, and as the plane was descending he was felt overwhelmed at the thought of reaching all these people. Get ready for a great illustration in a way that is classic Chuck Swindoll.

> Overwhelming odds can make cowards of us all…
>
> I'll never forget a story I read recently. A businessman and his wife took a few days of relaxation at an oceanfront hotel. One night a violent storm lashed the beach and sent massive breakers thundering against the shore.
>
> The wind finally died down, and shortly before daybreak the man slipped out of bed and took a walk along the beach to

see what damage had been done. As he strolled, he saw that the beach was literally covered with starfish that had been thrown ashore and helplessly stranded by the great waves. Once the morning sun would begin to burn through the clouds, the starfish would dry out and die.

Suddenly, the man saw an interesting sight. A young boy was picking up the starfish, one at a time, and flinging them back into the ocean.

"Why are you doing that?" the man asked the boy as he got close enough to be heard. "Can't you see that you'll never be able to get all those starfish back into the water? What difference can you make when there are just too many?"

The boy sighed as he picked up another starfish and tossed it into the water. Then as he watched it sink, he looked at the man, smiled, and said, "But I sure made a difference to that one." The businessman paused...and he also began picking up starfish!

True, one person cannot beat the odds. There will always be more people to reach than time or energy or commitment can provide. But the truth is that each one of us can touch a few. How wrong we would be to stop helping anyone because we cannot help everyone.

You can make a difference. And because you can...you must. Count on the Lord to honour and multiply your best efforts, even though they may seem small. Last time I checked, He was still rewarding faithfulness.[89]

This is what James 2:15–16 is talking about. It's not about helping the entire world, but rather helping those who enter your radar screen in day-to-day life.

Please don't misunderstand me: praying for others is very important, but if someone is hungry and you have the means to feed them, do it. It doesn't take a lot of time or resources to help someone out of a jam that might seem minor to you, but to them it could be the difference between life and death.

Out of our abundance, we must give to those less fortunate. You may never know who God has brought to you as you walk the paths of life.

Hebrews 13:1–2 says, *"Keep on loving one another as brothers and sisters. Do not forget to show hospitality to strangers, for by so doing some people have shown hospitality to angels without knowing it."* These messengers from God just might put you to the test, revealing the compassion you have for others in need.

Jesus gave a very candid description of helping others for His sake in Matthew 25:34–40:

> *Then the King will say to those on his right, "Come, you who are blessed by my Father, inherit the kingdom prepared for you from the foundation of the world. For I was hungry and you gave me food, I was thirsty and you gave me drink, I was a stranger and you welcomed me, I was naked and you clothed me, I was sick and you visited me, I was in prison and you came to me." Then the righteous will answer him, saying, "Lord, when did we see you hungry and feed you, or thirsty and give you drink? And when did we see you a stranger and welcome you, or naked and clothe you? And when did we see you sick or in prison and visit you?" And the King will answer them, "Truly, I say to you, as you did it to one of the least of these my brothers, you did it to me."* (ESV)

William MacDonald states it this way:

> The futility of words without deeds is now illustrated. We are introduced to two people. One has neither adequate daily food nor clothing. The other has both but is not willing to share them. Professing great generosity, the latter says to his poor brother, "Go and put on some clothing, and eat a good meal." But he doesn't raise a little finger to make this possible. What good are such words? They are positively worthless! They neither satisfy the appetite nor provide warmth for the body.[90]

Warren Wiersbe adds, "As believers, we have an obligation to help meet the needs of others, no matter who they may be. To help a person in need is an expression of love, and faith works by love."[91] Wiersbe then offers examples from God's Word:

> *Therefore, as we have opportunity, let us do good to all people, especially to those who belong to the family of believers.*
> —Galatians 6:10

> *If anyone has material possessions and sees a brother or sister in need but has no pity on them, how can the love of God be in that person? Dear children, let us not love with words or speech but with actions and in truth.*
> —1 John 3:17–18

This should be as natural as breathing to the children of God, who live a life that will honour our King, Lord, and Saviour Jesus Christ.

Application. I've thought of four ways to apply this to our lives:

1. Actively seek out those in need within your range.
2. When you see a need, if you're capable, fill it.
3. Have a heart of compassion for those who are less fortunate.
4. Help others, which honours our King, Saviour, and Lord Jesus.

James 2:17 says, "*In the same way, faith by itself, if it is not accompanied by action, is dead.*"

Observation. I love the way James expresses himself in such a direct manner. This requires very little explanation. He fires a direct hit toward people of faith, making us accountable for our own actions. He plainly states that if we don't practice what we preach, our faith is dead!

I'm not sure about you, but that isn't what I want for my walk with God, who makes me alive with Christ. Chuck Swindoll sums up the verse this way:

Faith and works go together like legs and the top of a table. You can't have a table without legs. Take away the legs and you're on the floor. You don't have genuine faith if works aren't right there along with it. They validate faith. That's the whole point of James's remark: Faith must be in partnership with works. They go together. They don't exist alone. If there is genuine faith in a person's life, then it will produce works of compassion and a deep care for the needs of others.

For a person who has been born again, there will be good deeds worked out in their life. But if a life shows no fruit, the person may not be born again. From our perspective this can seem subjective. But God sees clearly.[92]

John MacArthur adds, "Just as professed compassion without action is phony, the kind of faith without works is mere empty profession, not genuine saving faith."[93] This is reinforced in James 2:26, which says, *"As the body without the spirit is dead, so faith without deeds is dead."*

Just to be clear, James isn't talking about works saving you. William MacDonald clarifies this:

> A faith without works is not real faith at all. It is only a matter of words. James is not saying that we are saved by faith plus works. To hold such a view would be to dishonour the finished work of the Lord Jesus Christ. If we were saved by faith plus works, then there would be two saviours—Jesus and ourselves. But the New Testament is very clear that Christ is the one and only Savior. What James is emphasizing is that we are not saved by faith of words only but by the kind of faith which results in a life of good works. In other words, works are not the root of salvation but the fruit; they are not the cause but the effect.[94]

It is truly incredible to study the Bible using proper tools such as commentaries authored by great scholars of the Bible. Even a passage as short as this one amazes me with its enormous impact on our lives.

Practice What You Preach

The commentaries gleaned from these great authors also amaze me. Praise God for the people who have taken the time to dig deep into the Word of God. We are so blessed because of them.

To conclude this passage, Warren Wiersbe has some great thoughts to share:

> The person with dead faith has only an intellectual experience. In his mind, he knows the doctrines of salvation, but he has never submitted himself to God and trusted Christ for salvation. He knows the right words, but he does not back up his words with works. Faith in Christ brings life (John 3:16), and where there is life there must be growth and fruit. Three times in this paragraph, James warns that "faith without works is dead" (James 2:17, 20, 26). Beware of mere intellectual faith. No man can come to Christ by faith and remain the same anymore that he can come into contact with a 220-volt wire and remain the same. "He that hath the Son hath life; and he that hath not the Son of God hath no life." (1 John 5:12). Dead faith is not saving faith. Dead faith is counterfeit faith and lulls the person into a false confidence of eternal life.[95]

Isn't this a great summary of James 2:17?

Application. Here are three ways you can apply the truths in this passage:

1. As a believer in Jesus, you must act in such a way that shows the growth and fruit in your life, by doing good toward others for no other reason than your thankfulness for your salvation.
2. Make sure your words are backed up by your deeds.
3. Do not live a life that is defined by dead faith.

James 2:18 says, *"But someone will say, 'You have faith; I have deeds.' Show me your faith without deeds, and I will show you my faith by my deeds."*

Observation. This is probably the greatest verse in terms of defining the concept of practicing what you preach. As mentioned in the previous verse, faith alone is not what the Christian life is all about—you have to put it into practice.

Charles Ryrie explains the verse this way: "The challenger's statement ends before the word show. James's response begins there."[96] This is why you study the Bible: to know the truth that will set you free, that will give you a clear direction and understanding of what God wants from you.

A wonderful summary of this is found in 2 Peter 1:3–9:

> *His divine power has granted to us all things that pertain to life and godliness, through the knowledge of him who called us to his own glory and excellence, by which he has granted to us his precious and very great promises, so that through them you may become partakers of the divine nature, having escaped from the corruption that is in the world because of sinful desire. For this very reason, make every effort to supplement your faith with virtue, and virtue with knowledge, and knowledge with self-control, and self-control with steadfastness, and steadfastness with godliness, and godliness with brotherly affection, and brotherly affection with love. For if these qualities are yours and are increasing, they keep you from being ineffective or unfruitful in the knowledge of our Lord Jesus Christ. For whoever lacks these qualities is so nearsighted that he is blind, having forgotten that he was cleansed from his former sins.* (ESV)

I don't want the adjectives "ineffective and unfruitful" to be attached to me in the life Jesus has given me.

There are so many incredible scriptures to live by. How could we not be ambassadors for God and look for every opportunity to be there when someone needs not only daily provision, but ultimately a Saviour? John MacArthur puts it succinctly: "James' main point is the same: the only possible evidence of true faith is works."[97]

Some have said, "Preach the word every waking hour; use words when necessary." Your actions should speak much louder than your words. By doing so, people see who you are much more than they could by just hearing what you say.

William MacDonald has some poignant words on this subject:

True faith and good works are inseparable. James shows this by giving us a snatch from a debate between two men. The first man, who is genuinely saved, is the speaker. The second professes to have faith, but he does not demonstrate that faith by good works. The first is heard delivering an unanswerable challenge to the other. We might paraphrase the conversation: "Yes," the first man correctly and justifiably say, "you have faith, but you do not have works to demonstrate it. I claim that faith must be backed up by a life of works. Prove to me that you have faith without a life of good works. You cannot do it. Faith is invisible. The only way others can know you have faith is by a life that demonstrates it. I will show you my faith by my works." The key to this verse lies in the word show: To show faith apart from works is impossible.[98]

Application. Here the four ways in which you can apply this verse today:

1. Practice what you preach.
2. Live your faith through actions and good deeds. After meeting Jesus, there must be a difference in how you act.
3. Do not be an ineffective and unproductive Christian.
4. Honour Jesus for all He has done for you and never forget what you were saved from.

James 2:19 says, *"You believe that there is one God. Good! Even the demons believe that—and shudder."*
Observation. There are many who say, "I believe in God." The important question then remains: which god do you believe in? I once heard someone say, "Everyone believes in a god. Whatever you think about all the time, that is your god."

I remember the first time I heard that phrase like it was yesterday. My wife and I were attending a Bible study, and the comment shook me up. On the way home, I told my wife how hard that question had struck me, to the core of my soul. I certainly wasn't thinking about God all the time.

It always amazes me how God, through the prompting of the Holy Spirit, can grab hold of you and give you a shake. That night, I decided that I needed to saturate myself in God's Word and become a fully devoted follower of Jesus Christ.

In the Old Testament, Moses writes, *"Hear, O Israel: The Lord our God, the Lord is one. Love the Lord your God with all your heart and with all your soul and with all your strength"* (Deuteronomy 6:4–5). John MacArthur adds to this:

> You believe that God is one (ESV). A clear reference to the passage most familiar to his Jewish readers: the Shema (Deuteronomy 6:4–5), the most basic doctrine of the Old Testament. demons believe. Even fallen angels affirm the oneness of God and tremble at its implications. Demons are essentially orthodox in their doctrine (Matthew 8:29–30, Mark 5:7, Luke 4:41, Acts 19:15). But orthodox doctrine by itself is no proof of saving faith. They know the truth about God, Christ and the Spirit, but hate it and them.[99]

The scriptures which confirm James's comments about demons, according to MacArthur, are worth reviewing.

> *"What do you want with us, Son of God?" they shouted. "Have you come here to torture us before the appointed time?"*
> —Matthew 8:29

> *He shouted at the top of his voice, "What do you want with me, Jesus, Son of the Most High God? In God's name don't torture me!"*
> —Mark 5:7

> *Moreover, demons came out of many people, shouting, "You are the Son of God!" But he rebuked them and would not allow them to speak, because they knew he was the Messiah.*
> —Luke 4:41

These verses can be both very scary and extremely comforting for believers in Jesus. When you mess around with the world of darkness and demons, they can ruin your life. But take heart: we who are Christians understand that they live in fear of Jesus.

The incredible part of these passages is the fact that, as James states, the demons believe in God and shudder.

Charles Ryrie comments, "There is one God. The unity of God was a fundamental belief in Judaism, but if that belief did not produce good deeds it was no better than the monotheism of the demons."[100] William MacDonald makes a great point on this passage:

> A man's professed faith may be nothing more than mental assent to a well-known fact. Such intellectual agreement involves no committal of the person and does not produce a transformed life. It is not enough to believe in the existence of God. True, this is essential, but it is not sufficient. Even the demons believe in the existence of God and they shudder at the thought of their eventual punishment by Him. The demons believe the fact, but they do not surrender to the Person. This is not saving faith. When a person truly believes in the Lord, it involves a commitment of spirit, soul, and body. This commitment in turn results in a changed life. Faith apart from works is head belief, and therefore dead belief.[101]

Warren Wiersbe sums it up this way:

> The person with dead faith was touched only in his intellect: but the demons are touched also in their emotions. They believe and tremble. But it is not a saving experience to believe and tremble. A person can be enlightened in their mind and even stirred in their heart and be lost forever.[102] True saving faith involves something more, something that can be seen and recognized: a changed life. "Show me your faith without deeds," challenged James, "and I will show you my faith by what I do" (James 2:18). How could a person show faith without works?

Can a dead sinner perform good works? Impossible! When you trust Christ, you are "created in Christ Jesus to do good works which God has prepared in advance for us to do" (Ephesians 2:10). Being a Christian involves trusting Christ and living for Christ: you receive the life, then you reveal the life. Faith that is barren is not saving faith.[103]

As you can see, life in Christ involves a lot more than believing in God—and yet so many people's understanding stops here.

I'm thankful that anyone can come to Jesus for salvation in any state of mind or lifestyle and our Lord will accept them. However, after that a person's life must change.

Early on in this book, I mentioned one of the most frightening verses in all of Scripture, and I will repeat it here. Jesus was bringing the Sermon on the Mount to a close when He made these final statements:

> Not everyone who says to me, "Lord, Lord," will enter the kingdom of heaven, but only the one who does the will of my Father who is in heaven. Many will say to me on that day, "Lord, Lord, did we not prophesy in your name and in your name drive out demons and in your name perform many miracles?" Then I will tell them plainly, "I never knew you. Away from me, you evildoers!"
> —Matthew 7:21–23

The Christian life is far from easy, but it is a joyful and rewarding experience. And it is my hope that people will find Jesus and understand it to be so much more than just saying "I believe in God." As James 2:26 says, "As the body without the spirit is dead, so faith without deeds is dead."

Application. Here is one way in which you can apply this verse:

1. With the help of the Holy Spirit and God's Word, show others the truth about Jesus. It's far more than saying "I believe in God."

Practice What You Preach

As I reached the end of the book of James, I wanted to know what it was like to be the younger half-brother of Jesus Christ. James explained that he originally didn't believe Jesus was the Son of God, no matter what his parents or others had told him.

When he and Jesus had been young, the family was travelling home from Jerusalem after observing the Feast of the Passover—only to realize that they had left the twelve-year-old Jesus behind. They then had to return to the city, finding him in the Synagogue teaching, which James found rather strange (Luke 2:41–50).

It was also tough to have a brother who never did anything wrong.

"After my brother was crucified, I had as deep a feeling of sorrow as one could imagine," he told me. "But then He rose after three days. When I saw Him, I realized that He was the Son of God!"

That explains why James is so direct in his letter and teaching. It seems he was making up for lost time.

The Epistle of James is an important book in the Bible to study from cover to cover, as you can learn from it everything you need to understand life and spending eternity with Christ. To be taught by the half-brother of Jesus—who was with Him from a very young age, witnessed His crucifixion, and was with Him after He rose again—gives James some fairly impressive credentials.

Of all the people I have introduced you to from the Bible, James stands out to me as one of the most practical teachers. Hopefully, you will take up the challenge to not only study but also apply the book of James in your life. And most importantly, "Practice what you preach!"

- Chapter Nine -

Enduring Trials

In the last chapter, we spent some time with James. We'll now continue to examine his epistle as we discuss entering into the trials of life people encounter. When you walk with the Lord Jesus, that doesn't exclude you from encountering trials, but the main difference is that there is always hope to endure these trials.

You can be sure that as you grow in the Christian life, you'll run into trials and tribulations. Satan has nothing left in his arsenal except to discourage us through these negative circumstances.

When you look in the Old Testament, Job went through more trials than anyone could imagine, yet at the end of it, his faith in God was even stronger than it had been before. That's incredible! It's certainly worth reading the book of Job to see how Satan can attack us, and then read of the profundity of Job's encounter with Almighty God.

Let's take a look at another great passage from the Bible, and one that is extremely relevant for today:

> *Consider it pure joy, my brothers and sisters, whenever you face trials of many kinds, because you know that the testing of your faith produces perseverance. Let perseverance finish its work so that you may be mature and complete, not lacking anything. If any of you lacks wisdom, you should ask God, who gives generously to all without finding fault, and it will be given to you. But when you ask, you must believe and not doubt, because the one who doubts is like a wave of the sea, blown and tossed by the wind. That person*

should not expect to receive anything from the Lord. Such a person is double-minded and unstable in all they do…

Blessed is the one who perseveres under trial because, having stood the test, that person will receive the crown of life that the Lord has promised to those who love him.

—James 1:2–8, 12

As you can see from this passage, James is very direct in his teaching. These are important life lessons that will carry you through the really tough times you'll surely encounter.

As in the last chapter, James expects Christians to stand up and be counted, to take our walk with the Lord seriously, believe His promises, and lean on Him when there seems to be nowhere else to turn. When there's no hope in sight, we always have hope.

Let's start with James 1:2, which says, "*Consider it pure joy, my brothers and sisters, whenever you face trials of many kinds…*"

Observation. The first time I read this verse, I thought, *How in the world will I ever find joy when being hit with a trial in my life?* We will spend a lot of time on this verse, as it's filled with meanings that will give you an anchor to hang onto as these trials come. The commentaries have a lot to say on this matter and I'll be using them to discuss how to make it through when there seems to be no way out.

Be forewarned that this verse isn't for the faint of heart, and it takes great faith to trust Jesus in these difficult situations. The key is to understand what God is trying to teach you through the situations you're going through. Will you turn to God or take control and try to solve your trials on your own?

There are times when we have to go through the same trial over and over until God can get our attention. Sometimes it hurts. Hebrews 12:11 says, "*No discipline seems pleasant at the time, but painful. Later on, however, it produces a harvest of righteousness and peace for those who have been trained by it.*" This verse is all about training the Christian in the way of righteousness.

When I came to know Jesus as my Lord and Saviour, I imagined that life would be an easy road, that I would glide along for the rest of my earthly existence, eventually arriving in heaven. Though I hold firmly to the belief in the conclusion of my life in heavenly glory, the journey here and now is anything but easy.

John MacArthur once wrote a book titled *Hard to Believe*, and the title is a great description of the Christian life. The title doesn't mean that the Christian life is hard to understand, though; it refers to the fact that walking with the Lord on this earth isn't easy. It's a tough road, but with the help of the Holy Spirit we can find great joy while in the midst of great trials.

Philippians 3:1 tells us to *"rejoice in the Lord!"* And Philippians 4:4 says, *"Rejoice in the Lord always. I will say it again: Rejoice!"* MacArthur adds,

> This is the first time he adds, "in the Lord," which signifies the sphere in which the believer's joy exists—a sphere unrelated to the circumstances of life, but related to an unassailable, unchanging relationship to the sovereign Lord.[104]

MacArthur continues on to explain the phrase "count it all joy":

> The natural human response to trials is not to rejoice; therefore, the believer must make a conscious commitment to face them with joy. "trials." The Greek word connotes trouble, or something that breaks the pattern of peace, comfort, joy and happiness in someone's life. The verb form of this word means "to put someone or something to the test," with the purpose of discovering that person's nature or that thing's quality. God brings such tests to prove—and increase—the strength and quality of one's faith and to demonstrate its validity (James 1:2–12). Every trial becomes a test of faith designed to strengthen: if the believer fails the test by wrongly responding, that test becomes a temptation, or a solicitation to evil.[105]

So what's the deal with all this testing? Why do we have to go through it? Great question!

Chuck Swindoll explains this and gives us an understanding of what God is doing in our lives:

James tells us in the face of these troubles we are to find joy. Why? First, trials give us an opportunity to prove our faith in the Lord Jesus Christ. Second, trials have benefits for us. As we endure various trials, we find that they are all avenues that lead back to Jesus as we turn to Him for dependence. This in turn will strengthen our faith as we learn by depending on Christ that He is strong where we are weak. Remember there isn't any kind of pain we encounter that He has difficulty identifying with.[106]

Hebrews 4:15 reiterates, *"For we do not have a high priest who is unable to empathize with our weaknesses, but we have one who has been tempted in every way, just as we are—yet he did not sin."*
Warren Wiersbe adds,

Outlook determines outcome, and attitude determines action. God tells us to expect trials. It is not "if you will fall into various testings" but "when you fall into various testings." The believer who expects his Christian life to be easy is in for a shock. Jesus warned His disciples, "In the world you shall have tribulation" (John 16:33). Paul told his converts that "we must through much tribulation enter into the kingdom of God." (Acts 14:22). We cannot expect everything to go our way. Some trials come simply because we are human—sickness, accidents, disappointments, even seeming tragedies. Other trials come because we are Christians. Peter emphasizes this in his first letter when he says, "Beloved, think it not strange concerning the fiery trial which is to try you, as though some strange thing happening to you" (1 Peter 4:12). Satan fights us, the world opposes us, and this makes for a life of battle. Our values determine our evaluations; if we value comfort more than character, then trials will upset us. If we value the material and physical more than the spiritual, we will not be able to "count it all joy". If we live only for the present and forget the future, then trials will make us bitter, not better. So, when trials come, immediately give thanks to God and adopt a joyful attitude. Do not pretend; do not try self-hypnosis; simply look at trials through the eyes of faith. Outlook determines outcome; to end with joy, begin with joy. Sometimes we are looking at the wrong side of life; only the Lord sees the finished pattern. Let's not judge Him or His work from what we see today. His work is not finished yet![107]

William MacDonald explains,

These temptations are what we might call holy trials or problems which are sent by God and which test the reality of our faith and produce likeness to Christ. In verses 13–17, on the other hand, the subject is unholy temptations, which come from within, and which lead to sin. The Christian life is filled with problems. They come uninvited and unexpected. Sometimes they come singly and sometimes in droves. They are inevitable. James does not say "if we fall into various trials" but "when". We can never get away from them. The question is, "What are we going to do about them?" There are several possible attitudes we can take toward these testings and trials of life. We can rebel against them by adopting a spirit of defiance, boasting that we will battle through to victory by our own power. On the other hand, we can lose heart or give up under pressure. This is nothing but fatalism. It leads to questioning even the Lord's care for us. Again, we can grumble and complain about our troubles. Another option—we can indulge in self-pity, thinking of no one but ourselves, and trying to get sympathy from others. Or better, we can be exercised by the difficulties and perplexities. We can say, in effect, God has allowed this trial to come to me. He has some good purpose in it for me. I don't know what the purpose is, but I'll try to find out. I want His purposes worked out in my life. Don't rebel! Don't faint! Rejoice! These problems are not enemies, bent on destroying you. They are friends which have come to aid you to develop Christian character.[108]

Enduring Trials

I will conclude this discussion with something Jesus says in John 16:33: "*I have told you these things, so that in me you may have peace. In this world you will have trouble. But take heart! I have overcome the world.*"

As I write this, I'm facing some major trials in my life. I can tell you that while studying this verse, I have received a truly amazing amount of peace. When trials come close to home, they can be devastating and cripple you—if you let them.

I once heard someone pray like this, and I now repeat it a lot during my personal prayer time: "Lord, I surrender my life and those I love to Your care. Your will be done."

Again, there is great peace to be found in this verse. May it be the same for you.

Application. Considering this verse will carry you through a lot of unusual times in your life, I have a longer list of applications than normal:

1. Be prepared to face trials. They are coming.
2. Learn from and be trained by your trials.
3. Make a conscious decision to face your trials with joy.
4. Embrace trials, as they will strengthen your faith.
5. Lean on Jesus, not yourself, during trials.
6. Value character more than comfort.
7. Live for eternity, not for today.
8. View your trials through the eyes of faith.
9. Realize that your outlook will determine your outcome. In other words, to end with joy, begin with joy.
10. When a trial comes, ask yourself what you're going to do about it and what purpose God has for your situation.

The big question for me was, why? What was God's purpose for bringing these trials into my life? The next verse provides a very clear answer. Don't you just love the Word of God? It's always consistent, always has a plan, and always offers direction from God.

James 1:3–4 says, "*…because you know that the testing of your faith produces perseverance. Let perseverance finish its work so that you may be mature and complete, not lacking anything.*"

Observation. Sometimes it's difficult to understand why God would put us through trials and tests and then expect us to be pleased about them. You have to know that God has a reason for everything. After becoming a Christian, everything that happens to you helps prepare you for the day you will arrive in heaven. When we pray, "*[Y]our will be done, on earth as it is in heaven*" (Matthew 6:10), we're saying that we want our lives to reflect His heavenly will no matter where we are.

While on our journey of life, we must submit every area to God's purposes, plans, and glory. We can be certain that if God is putting us through something and we appear to be entering a vortex, we'll be stronger coming out the other end if we trust and lean on Jesus.

In this particular case, we're being trained in the area of perseverance—although some translations use the words patience, endurance, or steadfast. *The New Illustrated Bible Dictionary* defines perseverance as "the steadfast effort to follow God's commands and to do His work."[109]

The New Testament makes it clear that faith alone can save, but it's made equally clear that perseverance in doing good works is the greatest indication that a person's faith is genuine.[110] Indeed, perseverance springs from one's faithful trust that God has been steadfast toward His people.

Through persevering in God's work, Christians prove their deep appreciation for God's saving grace (1 Corinthians 15:57–58). As a result of perseverance, Christians can expect not only to enhance the strength of the church, but also to build up their strength of character. As Romans 5:3–4 tells us, "*Not only so, but we also glory in our sufferings, because we know that suffering produces perseverance; perseverance, character; and character, hope.*"

In short, Christians can expect to grow closer to God. They learn that they can persevere primarily because God is intimately related to them, and especially because they have the assurance of a final reward in heaven. 1 John 5:13 says, "*I write these things to you who believe in the name of the Son of God so that you may know that you have eternal life.*"

Beginning with James 1:3, we are told that "*because you know that the testing of your faith produces perseverance.*" Further, 1 Peter 1:7 speaks of trials in this way: "*These have come so that the proven genuineness of your faith—of greater worth than gold, which perishes even though refined by fire—may result in praise, glory and honor when Jesus Christ is revealed.*"

William MacDonald explains the testing of your faith:

> James pictures faith as a precious metal which is being tried by God to see if it is genuine. The metal is subjected to the fires of persecution, sickness, suffering, or sorrow. Without problems we would never develop perseverance.[111]

Hebrews 10:35–36 affirms, "*So do not throw away your confidence; it will be richly rewarded. You need to persevere so that when you have done the will of God, you will receive what he has promised.*"

John MacArthur adds, "Testing means proof or proving. Through tests, a Christian will learn to withstand tenaciously the pressure of a trial until God removes it at his appointed time, and even cherish the benefit."[112]

Warren Wiersbe asks some great questions and gives this response:

> What do Christians know that makes it easier to face trials and benefit from them? Faith is always tested. When God called Abraham to live by faith, He tested him in order to increase his faith. God always tests us to bring out the best; Satan tempts us to bring out the worst. The testing of our faith proves that we are truly born again. Trials work for the believer not against him. Paul said, "And we know that all things work together for good" (Romans 8:28). Trials, rightly used, help us to mature. What does God want to produce in our lives? Patience, endurance, and the ability to keep going when things get tough. In the Bible, patience is not a passive acceptance of circumstances, it is a courageous perseverance in the face of suffering and difficulty. The only way to develop perseverance and character in our lives is through trials. Endurance cannot be attained by reading a book (even this one), listening to a sermon, or even praying a prayer. We must go through the difficulties of life, trust God, and obey Him. The result will be perseverance and character. Knowing this, we can face trials joyfully. We know what trials will do in us and for us, and we know the end result will bring glory to God.[113]

Application. Here are four areas of application for this verse:

1. Prove your genuine faith by receiving trials joyfully.
2. Use trials to increase your faith. God uses them for your good.
3. With patience and endurance, keep going when life gets tough.
4. Trust God in the midst of your trials and obey Him.

James 1:4 says, *"Let perseverance finish its work so that you may be mature and complete, not lacking anything."*

Observation. When we go through trials and troubles in our lives, God hasn't left us. Such circumstances bring us into a form of boot camp, where things can be very unpleasant and extremely uncomfortable.

So why do we have to go through this? God wants only the best for us and our walk with the Lord doesn't stand still. Christianity isn't a dormant lifestyle; it is dynamic and always moving. With God's grace, we will move forward and grow—or in our own strength, we will stop and become stagnant, or go backwards. It amazes me how often we try to do things in our own power and strength.

This word, perseverance, is vital to our growth and essential to our boot camp training. This is one of those words that takes a second to say and a lifetime to achieve. When you use words like perseverance, patience, endurance, and steadfastness, be prepared to undergo a process of continual improvement. Don't be discouraged by the time it takes. I love the end of James 1:4, which states that we won't lack for anything. That's a fairly decent return on investment and it's certainly worth the effort!

We will always face struggles in life, but perseverance will help us mature and not get bogged down in the garbage, attempting to solve the unsolvable. Rather than losing sleep and not being able to concentrate on anything but what's standing in front of you, trust in God and work diligently to learn from the life lesson that's being taught. Through this process, you can find joy as opposed to sadness and discouragement.

You can be sure that Satan is going to be right there beside you to make you second-guess your decision to trust in Jesus and be led by the

Holy Spirit. 1 Peter 5:8 says, *"Be alert and of sober mind. Your enemy the devil prowls around like a roaring lion looking for someone to devour."* If any verse in the Bible should make you stand up and take notice, it's this one.

Understand that you can expect resistance, but God has overcome Satan and we must lean totally on Him. This doesn't mean that once we're mature, life will be perfect. James 3:2 says, *"We all stumble in many ways. Anyone who is never at fault in what they say is perfect, able to keep their whole body in check."*

John MacArthur explains, "Perfect. Not a reference to sinless perfection, but to spiritual maturity. The testing of faith drives believers to deeper communion and greater trusts in Christ—qualities that in turn produce a stable, godly, and righteous character."[114]

1 Peter 5:10 says, "And the God of all grace, who called you to his eternal glory in Christ, after you have suffered a little while, will himself restore you and make you strong, firm and steadfast." What a great promise!

We must always remember that we also play a part in this training. As Warren Wiersbe puts it,

> God cannot build character without our cooperation. If we resist Him, then He chastens us into submission. But if we submit to Him, then He can accomplish His work. He is not satisfied with a halfway job. God wants a perfect work; He wants a finished product that is mature and complete.
>
> God builds character before He calls to service; He must work in us before He can work through us. God spent twenty-five years working in Abraham before He could give him the promised son. God worked thirteen years in Joseph's life, putting him through 'various testing' before He could put him on the throne of Egypt. He spent eighty years preparing Moses for forty years of service. Our Lord took three years training His disciples, building their character. But God cannot work in us without our consent—there must be a surrendered will. The mature person does not argue with God's will; instead, he accepts it willingly and obeys it joyfully. God uses trials to wean

us away from childish things; but if we do not surrender to Him, we will become even more immature.[115]

So, as you can see, there is no quick fix. God will take us through a journey, and it can be a joyful trip or a very long and tiring excursion. From my standpoint, it's incredible to watch God work in my life. I truly feel great joy when a new lesson is learned!

William MacDonald explains it this way:

> We should not short-circuit the development of endurance in our lives. By cooperating with God, we become mature, well rounded Christians, lacking in none of the graces of the Spirit. We should never become despondent and discouraged when passing through trials. No problem is too great for our Father. Some problems in life are never removed. We must learn to accept them and to prove His grace sufficient. Paul asked the Lord three times to remove a physical infirmity. The Lord did not remove it but gave Paul the grace to bear it (2 Corinthians 12:8–10). Peace comes through submission to the will of God. Some problems in life are removed when we have learned our lessons from them. As soon as the Refiner (God) sees His reflection in the molten metal, He turns off the heat. Most of us lack wisdom to view the pressure of life from God's standpoint. We adopt a short-range view, occupying ourselves with immediate discomfort. We forget that God's unhurried purpose is to enlarge us through pressure.[116]

God isn't finished with us; we are a work in progress, and that process takes a lifetime. We aren't in trouble when trials come; we are in training. But in times of trouble, you have two choices: enjoy the ride or fight against it.

Isn't it great to know that the final outcome is heaven? God is truly trying to teach us how to get a taste of heaven on earth. The joy of the Lord is my strength!

Application. Here are four ways to apply this verse to your life:

1. Stay away from childish, immature things and conflicts.
2. Build character through perseverance with the help of our Lord Jesus.
3. Submit to the Lord so He may complete His work in you.
4. Learn to live with God's grace when it comes to the issues He chooses not to remove.

James 1:5 says, *"If any of you lacks wisdom, you should ask God, who gives generously to all without finding fault, and it will be given to you."*

Observation. When you study God's Word, it doesn't take much time to realize that the wisest person who ever lived was King Solomon, the son of David. When Solomon became King, God asked him a question in a dream: *"At Gibeon the Lord appeared to Solomon during the night in a dream, and God said, 'Ask for whatever you want me to give you'"* (1 Kings 3:5). Can you imagine the Creator of the universe asking you that question?

You're dealing with God. There is no request that cannot be granted. Anything, and I mean anything, is available.

What are some things I would like to have in my life? A long life, a perfect family, to coach an NFL football team, to be a professional golfer… and let's throw in a private jet. I mean, my list would be endless! Perhaps you're not as shallow as I am and have a much more spiritual list. Nonetheless, those are the things that come to mind for me—obviously, I'm not the wisest man in the world.

So how does Solomon answer? 1 Kings 3:9 says, *"So give your servant a discerning heart to govern your people and to distinguish between right and wrong. For who is able to govern this great people of yours?"* Wow! His answer was so much better than mine would have been!

God then responded, in 1 Kings 3:10–13:

It pleased the Lord that Solomon had asked this. And God said to him, "Because you have asked this, and have not asked for yourself long life or riches or the life of your enemies, but have asked for yourself understanding to discern what is right, behold, I now do according to your word. Behold, I give you a wise and discerning mind, so that none like you has been before you and none like you shall arise after you. I give you also what you have not asked, both riches and honor, so that no other king shall compare with you, all your days. (ESV)

It is apparent that Solomon certainly had the correct answer to that question.

All this reminds me of something Jesus said in the Sermon on the Mount regarding worry: *"But seek first his kingdom and his righteousness, and all these things will be given to you as well"* (Matthew 6:33). As Solomon did, we need to put God first and seek to honour Jesus—that is our mission in life as a Christian.

Other Scriptures reinforce the importance of asking for wisdom. Proverbs 2:6 says, *"For the Lord gives wisdom; from his mouth come knowledge and understanding."* When David was lamenting over his sin with Bathsheba, he looked to God for wisdom deep in his heart, crying out, *"Yet you desired faithfulness even in the womb; you taught me wisdom in that secret place"* (Psalm 51:6).

Asking for wisdom is a good thing! When your life runs off the tracks, God's wisdom through His Word will get you back on track. Matthew 7:7 says, *"Ask and it will be given to you; seek and you will find; knock and the door will open to you."* What an amazing feeling it is to know we are not alone.

William MacDonald puts it this way:

> We don't have to face the problems of life in our own wisdom. If, in the time of trial, we lack spiritual insight, we should go to God and tell Him all about our perplexity and ignorance. All who are thus exercised to find God's purpose in the trials will be liberally rewarded. And they need not worry that God will scold them either; He is pleased when we are teachable and tractable. We all lack wisdom. The Bible does not give specific answers to the innumerable problems that arise in life. It does not solve problems in so many words, but God's word does give us general principles. We must apply these principles to problems as they arise day to day. This is why we need wisdom.

Spiritual wisdom is the practical application of our Lord's teachings to everyday situations.[117]

John MacArthur writes,

Wisdom. James' Jewish audience recognized this as the understanding and practical skills that were necessary to live life to God's glory. It was not a wisdom of philosophical speculation, but the wisdom contained in the pure and peaceable absolutes of God's will revealed in his word and lived out. Only such divine wisdom enables believers to be joyous and submissive in the trials of life. "Ask God" This command is a necessary part of the believer's prayer life. God intends that trials will drive believers to greater dependency on him, by showing them their own inadequacies. As with all riches, God has wisdom in abundance available for those who seek it.[118]

Warren Wiersbe adds,

The people to whom James wrote had problems with their praying. When we are going through God-ordained difficulties, what should we pray about? James gives the answer: ask God for wisdom. We need wisdom so we will not waste the opportunities God is giving us to mature. Wisdom helps us understand how to use these circumstances for our good and God's glory.[119]

This passage from James 1:5 implores us not to find fault. Isn't it incredible that when you come to the Lord and ask for something, He doesn't make you look like a fool?

Early in my career, in one of my first management meetings, I recall the vice president of the company made a presentation and spoke a word I didn't understand. I raised my hand and asked him what the word meant, and he gladly told me before continuing on with his presentation.

After the meeting, my supervisor called me aside and, with a smirk on his face, asked if I was embarrassed for having made a fool out of myself in front of the entire management team. I explained that if the topic was important enough for the VP to present it, I wanted to make sure I knew what he was talking about. At first I felt bad, but then I thought, *How else am I going to learn?* Life is certainly an exercise in continual education.

It's funny how things work. I ended up taking over management of the region while that supervisor was let go from the company. When I was promoted, the VP I had questioned in that meeting told me that one of the things he liked about me was the fact that I'd asked that question. He applauded my integrity and courage for asking it.

I have to tell you, that certainly wasn't the outcome I expected. It's great to know that God loves our questions and will go above and beyond to show us His will through His Word. He will never make us feel bad for asking a question.

Application. I've listed three ways to apply this verse to your life:

1. When trials come, pray for wisdom so that you don't waste what God is trying to teach you.
2. Before making any major decision, ask God for wisdom.
3. Ask God to reveal His Word to you and have the wisdom to listen and live it.

James 1:6–8 says,

> *But when you ask, you must believe and not doubt, because the one who doubts is like a wave of the sea, blown and tossed by the wind. That person should not expect to receive anything from the Lord. Such a person is double-minded and unstable in all they do.*

Observation. In a previous chapter, I discussed that we should practice what we preach. This is very true with regard to faith and belief. Is Jesus the Lord of your life or not? Is Jesus your Saviour or not? Is Jesus who He said He was?

John MacArthur once preached a message titled "Jesus: Liar, Lunatic, or Lord?" which drove home the point that Jesus was either who He said He was, or He wasn't.[120] This is the core of our faith, and it's what separates Christianity from all the world's other religions. When people from certain religions claim that Jesus was either a prophet or a good man, they are directly opposing the claims from His own mouth. According to Jesus, He rose from the grave. Therefore, we serve a risen Saviour.

We have a relationship, not a religion. No other religion can make such a bold statement—that is why Jesus said in John 14:6, *"I am the way and the truth and the life. No one comes to the Father except through me."*

I say all this to encourage you to understand that when you ask for wisdom, you should have no doubt about it in your heart and mind. You have to be all-in for Jesus; this isn't a time for flipflopping around. You're coming into the presence of the Almighty God, who can do anything. Hebrews 11:1 says, *"Now faith is confidence in what we hope for and assurance about what we do not see."* Doubt is going back and forth on what you believe or don't believe.

John MacArthur confirms the truth conveyed in this verse:

> Ask in faith. Prayer must be offered with confident trust in a sovereign God... with no doubt. This refers to having one's thinking divided within itself, not merely because of mental indecision but an inner moral conflict or distrust in God. Wave of the sea. The person who doubts God's ability or willingness to provide this wisdom is like the blowing, restless sea, moving back and forth with its endless tides, never able to settle.[121]

As usual, John MacArthur hits the nail on the head.

I'm always amazed at the depth of each verse of God's Word, and even more amazed at the Bible scholars who dig so deeply into each word.

William MacDonald adds another take on this verse:

> We must approach God in faith, without doubting. We must believe He loves and cares, and that nothing is impossible with

Him. If we doubt His goodness and His power, we will have no stability in times of trouble.[122]

Warren Wiersbe says, "James compares the doubting believer to the waves of the sea, up one minute and down the next."[123]

James 1:7, the next segment of this passage, says, *"That person should not expect to receive anything from the Lord."* Again, please note that James pulls no punches in his epistle.

The more I live my life as a Christian, the more I realize that consistency and faith are the major keys to succeeding in our walk with the Lord. Don't be discouraged when you stumble in any area of your life. We serve a God of grace and mercy, so just get back in the game.

The message here is to live a life that is obedient and honouring to God. And with the help of the Holy Spirit, be as consistent as possible. I praise the Lord that we aren't thrown away for our mistakes in life. God will always chasten us when necessary and reward us for our obedience.

This is quite a verse! None of the commentaries offer much elaboration, and none of my study Bibles have corresponding verses. This is a first for me. Basically, what is said is very clear and requires little explanation. One thing is certain: I would not want to be that person who lives a life of continual indecision.

James 1:8 declares, *"Such a person is double-minded and unstable in all they do."* James takes a dim view of jumping in and out of our faith in Jesus. Charles Ryrie calls this a "man of divided allegiance."[124] Psalm 119:113 says, *"I hate double-minded people, but I love your law."*

These people are also described in 2 Peter 2:14: *"With eyes full of adultery, they never stop sinning; they seduce the unstable; they are experts in greed—an accursed brood!"* It appears Peter isn't fond of this type of individual either. He continues his disdain:

> *He [Paul] writes the same way in all his letters, speaking in them of these matters. His letters contain some things that are hard to understand, which ignorant and unstable people distort, as they do the other Scriptures, to their own destruction.*
> —2 Peter 3:16

What Peter describes is the way Paul wrote the scripture, but false teachers distorted them.

John MacArthur writes,

> A literal translation of the Greek expression that denotes having one's mind or soul divided between God and the world (James 4:4 relates with, "You adulterous people, don't you know that friendship with the world is hatred toward God? Anyone who chooses to be a friend of the world becomes an enemy to God"). This man is a hypocrite, who occasionally believes in God but fails to trust Him when trials come, thereby receiving nothing. The use of this expression in James 4:8 makes it clear that it refers to an unbeliever ("Come near to God and he will come near to you. Wash your hands, you sinners, and purify your hearts, you double-minded").[125]

Warren Wiersbe adds,

> This is the experience of the double-minded person. Faith says, "Yes!" but unbelief says, "No!" Then doubt comes along and says "Yes!" One minute and "No!" the next. It was doubt that made Peter sink in the waves as he walked toward Jesus in Matthew 14:22–33. Jesus asked him, "You of little faith, why did you doubt?" When Peter started his walk of faith, he kept his eyes on Christ, but when he was distracted by the wind and waves, he ceased to walk by faith; he began to sink. He was double-minded, and he almost drowned.[126]

Application. There are a lot of ways we can apply this passage to our lives:

1. Pray with assurance for God's will to be done.
2. Pray with a faithful heart knowing that Jesus is faithful.
3. Never doubt God. He's got this!
4. Pray to have the faith to surrender everything to the Lord.

5. Ask for the Lord's help to keep your eyes on Jesus.
6. Choose God, not the world. Don't be a hypocrite.
7. Do your best not to vacillate when it comes to your faith.

James 1:12 says, *"Blessed is the one who perseveres under trial because, having stood the test, that person will receive the crown of life that the Lord has promised to those who love him."*

Observation. Thankfully, there is hope. Through the assistance of the Holy Spirit, we will get through to the other side of our troubles, and we will be blessed if we persevere.

As if heaven wasn't enough for lost sinners, God also provides an opportunity to receive a crown. Please understand that salvation alone and being saved from eternal damnation is more than anyone could ever receive.

So what is the "crown of life"? Why do we have to endure these trials that God allows to come into our lives in the first place?

These are tough questions that need to be answered.

While studying this verse, I found that Warren Wiersbe had great answers to both:

> Paul often used athletic illustrations in his letters, and James does so here. He is not saying that the sinner is saved by enduring trials. He is saying that the believer is rewarded by enduring trials. How is he rewarded? First, by growth in Christian character. This is more important than anything else. He is rewarded also by bringing glory to God and by being granted a crown of life when Jesus Christ returns. First the crown, then the cross. First, the suffering, then the glory. God does not help us by removing the tests, but by making the tests work for us. Satan wants to use the tests to tear us down, but God uses them to build us up. In James 1:12, James used a very important word, love. We would expect him to write, "the crown of life, which the Lord has promised to them that trust Him" or "that obey Him." Why did James use love? Because love is the spiritual motivation behind every imperative in this section. Why do we have a joyful attitude as we face trials? Because

we love God, and He loves us, and He will not harm us. Why do we have an understanding mind? Because He loves us and has shared His truth with us, and we love Him in return. Why do we have a surrendered will? Because we love Him. Where there is love there is surrender and obedience. Why do we have a believing heart? Because love and faith go together. When you love someone, you trust him, and you do not hesitate to ask for help. God's purpose for trials is maturity.[127]

Wiersbe certainly gives us a clear account of why we face such trials. He also covers the opportunity we are given to grow in our faith and show the Lord that our lives are His; we are not our own, we are bought with a price, and we therefore honour God with our bodies.

John MacArthur adds an excellent description of the crown:

Crown of life. Best translated "the crown that is life." "Crown" was the wreath put on the victor's head after ancient Greek athletic events. Here, it denotes the believer's ultimate reward, eternal life, which God promised to him and will grant in full at death or at Christ's coming.[128]

2 Timothy 4:8 says, "*Now there is in store for me the crown of righteousness, which the Lord, the righteous Judge, will award to me on that day—and not only to me, but also to all who have longed for his appearing.*" 1 Peter 5:4 affirms, "*And when the Chief Shepherd appears, you will receive the crown of glory that will never fade away.*"

For those who feel that the journey is over once you receive Jesus as your Lord and Saviour, you are greatly mistaken. As mentioned earlier, John MacArthur wrote a book titled *Hard to Believe*, and I would strongly recommend Christians read this incredible book. Christianity isn't for the faint of heart or weak people looking for an anchor to cling to. It is a vibrant, exciting journey that has an awesome ending!

Those who receive the gifts of God and just sit on them, waiting for heaven to come, miss out on so much. Yes, we face trials, and yes, we go through very tough days, but we also have days that can only be described as euphoric, as God uncovers His plans for us.

Please take a serious look at these verses, written by Paul. They talk about our walk with the Lord after salvation:

> *By the grace God has given me, I laid a foundation as a wise builder, and someone else is building on it. But each one should build with care. For no one can lay any foundation other than the one already laid, which is Jesus Christ. If anyone builds on this foundation using gold, silver, costly stones, wood, hay or straw, their work will be shown for what it is, because the Day will bring it to light. It will be revealed with fire, and the fire will test the quality of each person's work. If what has been built survives, the builder will receive a reward. If it is burned up, the builder will suffer loss but yet will be saved—even though only as one escaping through the flames.*
> —1 Corinthians 3:10–15

William MacDonald sums it up this way:

> There is no suggestion, of course, that eternal life is the reward for enduring testing, but those who have endured with fortitude will be honoured for that kind of life, and will enjoy a deeper appreciation of eternal life in heaven.[129]

Application. Here are three ways you can apply this verse to your life:

1. Work daily to turn your trials into joy, knowing that God has a plan for you.
2. Show your love for Jesus in everything you do or experience. He died for you!
3. Build on the cornerstone of your salvation and persevere for God with all your heart.

I would like to bring this chapter to a conclusion with some great questions written by William MacDonald:

Now let us make this section on holy trials practical in our own lives. How do we react when various forms of testing come into our lives? Do we complain bitterly against our misfortunes of life, or do we rejoice and thank the Lord for them? Do we advertise our trials, or do we bear them quietly? Do we live in the future, waiting for our circumstances to improve, or do we live in the present, seeking to see the hand of God in all that comes to us? Do we indulge in self-pity and seek sympathy, or do we submerge self in a life of service for others?[130]

What a great way to conclude a chapter on enduring trials! May God use His Word to change our patterns and worldly attitudes towards life and learn to lean wholly on our Saviour.

- CHAPTER TEN -

THE BIBLE AND BUSINESS

Early on in my career, the general manager of the company I worked for noticed how enthusiastically I completed my work every day. One day he came up to me and asked, "How can you stay so positive and upbeat all the time?"

I was very new in my Christian life and had just started to read my Bible. That night, I went home and read Colossians 3:22 to 4:1—and that's where I would like to begin our study of the Bible and business.

When we get to our review of Colossians 3:23, I'll tell you how I answered the general manager's question.

Is it possible that the Bible actually does mean something in the business world? Is that even possible? I've been in business for a number of decades and can tell you without question that the Bible is the primary reason for any success I may have had in my career.

You've probably heard people say, "I'm a self-made person. I earned everything I have." Unfortunately, rarely do you see successful people give anyone but themselves credit for their many achievements.

The Old Testament, way back in the days of Moses, reveals a very telling fact:

> *You may say to yourself, "My power and the strength of my hands have produced this wealth for me." But remember the Lord your God, for it is he who gives you the ability to produce wealth, and so confirms his covenant, which he swore to your ancestors, as it is today.*
>
> —Deuteronomy 8:17–18

Warren Wiersbe stated, "There's peril in prosperity and comfort, for we may become so wrapped up in the blessings that we forget the One who gave us the blessings."[131]

Just a few verses before this, Moses tells his people not to forget where they came from.

Although Moses was referring to Egyptian bondage and slavery, the same principles apply to being rescued from the slavery of sin by our Lord Jesus Christ.

> *Otherwise, when you eat and are satisfied, when you build fine houses and settle down, and when your herds and flocks grow large and your silver and gold increase and all you have is multiplied, then your heart will become proud and you will forget the Lord your God, who brought you out of Egypt, out of the land of slavery.*
> —Deuteronomy 8:12–14

How incredible is that? Written literally thousands of years ago, it's as relevant today as it was in Moses's time.

So as you can see, the Bible is especially important in business. But I hope to show you some very practical ways God's Word can be used daily.

Before we go further, let me give you an overview of my career, and then we'll get into the role God's Word has played in it. My career was truly blessed—and believe me, I give all glory to Jesus for the success I had.

Shortly after I first became a Christian, I was working at a small building supply store, working exceptionally long hours and not making a lot of money. I couldn't see a bright future ahead of me. At the time, I was married with one child and had another on the way.

Well, I was fired from this job, for good reason, but that should give you an idea of my ability. I couldn't hold a job in a building supply store, and it struck me that it was time to take a serious look at my life. I could feel the Lord working in my heart and mind.

One day, after being unemployed for seven weeks, which seemed like a lifetime, I went into my bedroom, sank to my knees in prayer, and cried like a baby. I had nowhere to go and no future employment on the horizon.

Let me stress that at the time I was twenty-five years old and had a Grade Ten education. (Again, let me reiterate: complete your education!) I didn't have a stellar employment record.

The next morning, I received a phone call from the human resources manager of a company in the electrical industry. I had been interviewed for a job at this company, and there were two candidates. One had a college diploma, and the other was me.

They ended up hiring both of us. The person with the diploma was given a job in marketing and I was given a job in customer service. I made up my mind that I was going to work harder than I had ever done before and was going to make something out of this job.

Years later, I found out that the general manager had seen something in me and overruled his staff. The decision to hire me had been an executive decision.

What happened after that can only be described as miraculous, and there is no doubt in my mind that it was orchestrated by the Lord Jesus. The general manager took a keen interest in me and my career. I was truly blessed early in my career by this man who not only hired me but also became an incredible mentor and friend. I believe God brought this man into my life at the perfect time. He challenged me in areas of work, family and my walk with the Lord. I will be forever grateful for the impact Vince Nall had in my life. We became incredibly close friends, and even to this day, I thank God for bringing him into my life, as I wouldn't have accomplished anything close to what I have without his guidance and mentorship—and the fact that God had me in His sight.

One day while in the office, he asked me about my faith; he told me he had done some good things and some bad things, but on balance he felt that his works would get him to heaven. I'm surprised I made it through that meeting without getting fired, as I told him straight that his theory would end up leading him to hell. He then asked if I thought I was that good. I told him that I was unquestionably far from good, but I had been forgiven. I then illustrated this with a story I had heard in church.

Now picture the scene. I was in this man's office, pacing back and forth with a book in my hand, telling him about Jesus. The book wasn't a Bible, but it was meant to represent one. I was on fire for Jesus.

I suddenly picked up a chair and explained that this represented a sin. I then "sinned" again, picking up an object from his desk. The more I sinned, the more objects I picked up, to the point that I had to put the "Bible" down. I sinned some more, to the point that I couldn't continue pacing.

Then, in dramatic fashion, I asked forgiveness of my sin and with that threw all the items down, grabbed my Bible, and started pacing back and forth again.

I will never forget what happened next.

"If you can sell my product like that, I'll pay you $50,000 a year!" he exclaimed.

At the time, I was earning $12,000. At that moment, for one of the first times in my life, we discussed the plan of salvation together. This not only solidified our relationship; he began to mentor me. That certainly wasn't the outcome I had expected from that meeting.

During the days to follow, we spent hours in his office as he trained me and taught me business practices, sales techniques, and strategic planning that I still use today. He then explained the importance of education. Under his guidance, I went back to community college and took many industry and business courses.

But just sitting in his office was like attending university and majoring in the best business program available. As he mentored me, my salary increased, as did my position in the company. He met my family, and I met his, and we became remarkably close. He gave me advice on marriage and parenting, and he challenged my faith when I went off the rails. Aside from my own parents, no one was more influential in my life than this man.

Six months into my career, I was promoted to be the customer service manager. Thirteen months later, I was an outside salesman. This was a significant step up, as I was given a company vehicle. At the time I was driving an old Chevy Nova with a standard three-speed transmission with no radio. I now had a brand-new car, nine years newer, with not only a radio but air conditioning and power windows. In a year and a half, my business life had changed dramatically.

Well, I only kept that job for eleven months before I was promoted again, this time to the position of regional manager. In a span of two and a half years, I went from being unemployed and broke to becoming the regional manager of a major electrical manufacturer. I was only twenty-eight years old. Honestly, I was one of the youngest regional managers in the industry.

After sixteen years with this company, my mentor moved on to another company, and out of nowhere came a job opportunity in the same industry. This new company wanted to discuss the possibility of me taking on the position of vice president of sales and marketing.

I have a lot of friends in the industry, and we had a lot of fun together and played jokes on each other. When I was first contacted, I thought it was a joke.

"Sorry, I'm only interested in a president position," I replied.

I'll never forget what the human resources manager on the phone said: "There is no president here. This VP position reports to the headquarters in the United States."

I immediately realized this could be legit.

I'm amazed I even got an interview after that comment, but God was undoubtedly directing my life. I later found out that sixteen other people had been lined up for interviews for that VP job.

This is when I learned a great prayer from my brother: "Lord, if it is Your will for me to take this job, please open all the doors. If not, please close them."

I went into the interviews with incredible confidence, a confidence that could only come from God. I was straightforward with my answers and brutally honest.

Well, it got down to the final four candidates and the manager we would report to flew in for the last interviews.

There were four interviews in total, and I didn't take any of them during regular business hours. I hadn't felt it would be right to do that, while I was employed by someone else. This turned out to be a major point in my favour down the road.

When I met with the manager from the U.S., he made it clear from the beginning that this was a global organization and I would be required to relocate to another country within five years. Again, with the kind of confidence that can only come from the Lord, I told him that wasn't going to happen. In response, he just said that he had truly enjoyed meeting me.

He was about to conclude the interview when I asked him for a few extra minutes to talk about the job description. I explained that it was all wrong for this position and that I had rewritten it to make it more effective for the company, to increase revenues. He read the revised job description and I could see he was impressed. He asked if I was sure I wouldn't be willing to relocate. Again I said, "Not a chance."

Just as I was about to leave, I asked if I could leave him with two final thoughts. And before I reveal them, please remember that this happened during the era when personal computers were only starting to take off in a big way. Our industry was a little slow to get up to speed in this area.

"As I see it, there are two things wrong with this company," I said. "One, you have no desire to automate your sales force, something that would give you a strong competitive advantage. And two, *you*. I'm certain not many people would challenge you, and that's a problem. I would challenge you to take a serious look at the job description and sales automation."

He just stared at me and finally said, "Are you sure I can't convince you to relocate?"

I said no, thanked him for his time, and told him I had greatly enjoyed meeting him.

Just when I thought the story was over, I received a call from the company. The person on the other end of the line informed me that they wanted me to interview with the company's two other VPs, the ones running Operations and Finance.

It was now down to two candidates.

During the interview, I was extremely confident that God would either open the door or close it. So I was very enthusiastic and explained what I thought the company needed. Afterward, they thanked me for coming in.

"So are you going to recommend me?" I asked.

They just stared at me for a little while.

"Well, I'm not sure what I'm getting from the other candidate, but I certainly know what I'm getting from you," one of them said.

"That sounds good. Does that mean you're going to recommend me?"

One said he could not say, and the other said that he would.

Shortly after that, I received a call from the human resources manager with a question. The company wanted to know if they were in the ballpark, salary-wise, before making me a formal offer. When I heard the number, I nearly tell off my chair. I then confirmed that it was in line with my expectations.

The final stage in the recruitment process was to spend a day of tests and meetings with a business psychologist. Because I wouldn't meet during business hours, the psychologist had to meet me on a Saturday. This didn't bode well for me, and he asked if this was some type of ploy to show integrity. I just told him that by the end of the eight hours of testing, he would know the answer.

I had no idea where that response came from.

At one point, he came in while I was completing a test and asked if it was true that I hadn't attended university, since my answers reflected a university-level education. I was in shock and continued the test.

He then came in once more to comment that I had scored higher in sales ability than anyone else he had tested.

At the end of the day, as we were talking about the test results, he gave me an incredibly positive reading.

"Are you going to recommend me?" I asked.

He said, "I cannot say. However, your competitor is going to have to get an incredible score to beat you."

Three days later, I was offered the position. I remained in that position for twenty-five years and the company grew to three times its initial size from the time I took over.

So what happened to me? How do you go from termination at a building supply store to regional manager in two and a half years, only to become the vice president of an even larger organization? The only change in my life was Jesus and an amazing mentor. My confidence level was growing, as was my faith and knowledge of Jesus Christ.

One day thirty years ago, I had an incredible urge to not just read my Bible but understand what it says. You can learn an enormous amount just by reading the Bible, and studying it can be life-changing. What I found most interesting was how much the Bible talks about the way one should conduct themselves in business.

So, I asked Paul, "Does the Bible discuss business practices?"

He explained to me that the Bible goes into great detail on the topics of work ethic, honesty and integrity, your relationship to your supervisor, your reputation or testimony, and even your management skills and servant leadership. The Bible offers many insights into best practices for working, managing, and even running your own company. One of the most important traits you can develop in your career is a spirit of thankfulness and gratitude to God for the fact that you have a job and the ability to do it.

Paul then explained that he had written about slaves and masters in both Ephesians and Colossians. These principles can be applied to both employees and employers, since the concepts are the same.

As we journey through these passages, keep in mind that the term *slave* will be understood to mean *employee*, and the *master* will be *employer*.

At the end of the day, these practices will honour our Lord Jesus in the workplace.

I would like to begin at the start of my career and the verses that most impacted me over the years. The first passage to study has to do with integrity, which had an enormous impact on my life in the early years.

Colossians 3:22 says, *"Slaves, obey your earthly masters in everything; and do it, not only when their eye is on you and to curry their favor, but with sincerity of heart and reverence for the Lord."*

Observation. This first section states that you must obey your employer in everything, but we need to understand that never in Scripture would God suggest this in relation to disobedience to Him. Acts 5:29 asserts, *"Peter and the other apostles replied: 'We must obey God rather than human begins!'"* This is where integrity comes into play. If you find yourself in a compromising position, you have to stand up for what is right and God-honouring.

In my experience, it's rare to be asked to do something dishonest, but if you are, you need to take a stand—God will honour that. Simply put, this verse tells us that in the course of your daily work, you should listen to your supervisor and do what you're told.

> *Teach slaves to be subject to their masters in everything, to try to please them, not to talk back to them, and not to steal from them, but to show that they can be fully trusted, so that in every way they will make the teaching about God our Savior attractive.*
>
> —Titus 2:9–10

Through your actions toward your employer, as they observe your daily routine and work ethic, you may be the only "Bible" they ever read.

The next discussion is one that everyone should pay close attention to. I'm sure you've seen people at work who sit around and do as little as possible. Then, when the boss walks in, they immediately jump up and start working feverishly to make their supervisor think they're being diligent. But as soon as the boss leaves, they go right back to their old ways.

Some versions of the Bible call this "eyeservice." You never want to be one of these people, as it will test your integrity. These people will eventually be found out.

Colossians 3:22 also talks about currying favour. There's a common unsavoury term for people like this, the ones who overcompliment their supervisor, telling them how great they are and how much they admire them. For these people, Galatians 1:10 has an admonishment: *"Am I now trying to win the approval of human beings, or of God? Or am I trying to please people? If I were still trying to please people, I would not be a servant of Christ."*

On top of that, behind their supervisors' backs, these complimenters rip the very same people to shreds. This is even worse than "eyeservice." As appealing as it may be, don't participate in negative conversations about your supervisor—or anyone else at work, for that matter. This isn't the Christian employee that you want to be, as you will see by the next example.

There was a time in my career when I got involved with some of the managers in my peer group. There was going to be a change at the top of our organization, with a new person coming in to run the company. One of the managers was trying to get the job, and the other managers and I began to have negative discussions about this individual. It started out with a few comments and escalated into consuming an enormous amount of our time, effort, and thought. It progressed to the point that it seemed to be all I was thinking about, even interfering with my sleep.

One night at home, my wife wanted to know what was happening at work, as it was truly having an adverse effect on me. When I told her what I was doing, she gave me the best advice I've ever heard: "Why don't you just shut up and do your job?"

The next day, I called the managers into my office and apologized for getting involved in these conversations. It was amazing how much pressure this relieved, and I was quickly able to resume my efforts to build the business instead of tearing it down. This not only had made me look bad, but it was hurting my testimony. And it certainly did not honour God.

This is addressed in Ephesians 4:29: *"Do not let any unwholesome talk come out of your mouths, but only what is helpful for building others up according to their needs, that it may benefit those who listen."* If we could live that verse at work for the rest of their lives, and that verse alone, it would bless us beyond measure.

It still amazes me how a single verse in this incredible book can change your life forever.

You've probably heard the old expression that talks about wearing our hearts on our sleeves. That saying always comes to mind when this subject arises. Sincerity of the heart has to be practiced so that it becomes second nature to us. When you're upfront and honest in everything you do, life becomes very simple.

You may fool people, but you will never fool God; He knows your heart. As 1 Samuel 16:7 says, *"The Lord does not look at the things people look at. People look at the outward appearance, but the Lord looks at the heart."*

There's no issue with complimenting or encouraging your supervisor or fellow employees—as a matter of fact, it can be a great ministry. Just make sure that you truly mean it and it comes from the heart. It won't take long for you to gain a reputation as a sincere and honest person, and that will bode extremely well for you as your career moves forward. Not only will this honour God, but good things are bound to happen to you.

As a believer, you should take an interest in those around you—a sincere interest, not just a quick comment on an issue or when someone seems out of sorts. When you care for others, they will notice it, and this could open the door for you to eventually share your faith with them.

It's easy to ruin many weeks of compassion shown to others with one slipup. 2 Corinthians 11:3 says, *"But I am afraid that just as Eve was deceived by the serpent's cunning, your minds may somehow be led astray from your sincere and pure devotion to Christ."* Stay alert in your pursuit of a sincere heart to others—and if and when you slip up, ask for forgiveness. Remember this is not about you, it is about Jesus.

We require God's help to stay consistent in this, but remember that He is always with us as we learn and trust Him. Hebrews 10:22 advises us to *"draw near to God with a sincere heart and with the full assurance that faith brings."* When people think of you, pray that they look upon you as one who really and sincerely cares for others.

Colossians 3:22 then talks about having *"reverence for the Lord."* Well, that says it all. Revering God is our only reason for being.

For whatever reason, God has put you in your current place of employment and now it's your time to flourish for the Lord Jesus.

I am reminded of the passage in Matthew 6:33, where Jesus said, *"But seek first his kingdom and his righteousness, and all these things will be given to you as well."* It's difficult to imagine not prioritizing your career in the first place in your life, not working to make sure you can get the most out of your employment, to advance yourself, to get to the top, to become a workaholic. There's nothing wrong with having a strong work ethic and getting ahead in an organization, but our top priority must always be to seek God first. When you put the Lord first, as the passage instructs, career advancement may come, relationship and family will be stronger, you will come alive with Christ, and He will be there when trials come. God will bless your life when you honour Jesus.

This is a lesson I truly wish I could have learned early on in my career, and I hope this book will assist you in realizing the importance of this incredible passage so you can live it out long before I did.

Matthew 6:33 comes from the Sermon on the Mount and is part of a longer passage devoted to worrying. For years, I worried about job security, finances, family, friends, and housing, and tried to fix these things in my own power, forgetting that God is in control; when He leads our lives, everything is a lot easier and more joyful.

God's got this—if you put Him first right out of the gate. If not, you lose out on joy and allow Satan to rule in your life. Eventually, you'll realize that God is the only way. God loves us so much that He sent His one and only Son to save us. We have a holy God who created the universe and is always watching over us—so we should live a life remembering who He is. Never take for granted how important it is to revere the Most High God in our hearts and minds every day.

To return for a moment to the subject of dealing with your supervisor, let me add one final wrinkle. Ephesians 6:5 states, *"Slaves, obey your earthly masters with respect and fear, and with sincerity of heart, just as you would obey Christ."* We are to look upon our supervisors as we would look upon Jesus. Of course, they aren't going to live the life of Jesus, but we are nonetheless supposed to respect and obey them as we do Christ.

Application. There are four applications to take away from this verse:

1. Do your job without complaining and be respectful to your supervisor.
2. Do not participate in negative conversations about other employees.
3. Sincerely help and care for others when the opportunities arrive.
4. Put the Lord Jesus in first place in everything you do, and pray for wisdom.

The next verse is one of my favourite verses for a Christian in business. This is one that can make a huge difference in your success. I tried my best to live this one to the fullest.

Colossians 3:23 says, *"Whatever you do, work at it with all your heart, as working for the Lord, not for human masters…"*

Observation. At the beginning of this chapter, I mentioned that the general manager of my company asked me, "How can you stay so positive and upbeat all the time?" Well, I went home that night and read and reread the passage from Colossians 3:22 to 4:1, and the next day I met with him again. I had photocopied this passage of Scripture and handed it to him. I asked him to take special note of verse 23. We then had a great conversation, and this solidified my relationship with the man.

The verse advises us, "Whatever you do, work at it with all your heart…" Honestly, I enjoy life, and the life the Lord has given to me has been blessed beyond my wildest dreams. I get very excited about many things: marriage, family, home, friends, vacations, and the list goes on and on. The key to happiness is having Jesus at the centre of my life. When you work with all your heart and are enthusiastic and energetic, good things start to happen. Work begins to be fun!

My passion was for making presentations, and this was the skill that made my career really blossom. I showed great enthusiasm. A fun way to look at the meaning of *enthusiasm* is found in the last four letters, IASM, which I think of as an acronym for I Am Sold Myself. That's a great definition, because if you believe in what you're presenting—whether it be in business or ministry—the more passion you will radiate.

Enthusiasm is great, but there has to be depth to it, and the key is knowing what you're going to say through preparation and study. Not only should you prepare, but you should deliver the message wholeheartedly. Work won't feel like work when you do it with this in mind.

The second part of this verse deals with who you're working for—"*as working for the Lord, not for human masters.*" Chuck Swindoll wrote, "Do you respect your employer or display a bad attitude? Do you work hard? With enthusiasm? Remember that even in an employee role, your ultimate reward comes from God, not your employer."[132] This is a tough one, as you need to look at your employer as if they are the Lord.

This reinforces the earlier point in Colossians 3:22, which talks about revering the Lord in our work. Eventually, your main purpose should be to make your supervisor successful. When you gain a reputation for putting your boss first, they will notice. This may or may not advance your career, but others will see the difference you make as a Christian employee. This may be the one thing that one day gives someone the opportunity to come to Jesus.

If you think you always have to reach for the top of your career, this sentiment will hinder your advancement. But please note what Jesus said about being number one. As the disciples were arguing about who should be the greatest, He said, *"Anyone who wants to be first must be the very last, and the servant of all"* (Mark 9:35 reveals). It's all about Jesus!

Application. Here are three ways you can apply this in your life today:

+ Work enthusiastically at whatever you do.
+ Treat your supervisor as if he was the Lord.
+ Keep in mind that it's all about Jesus.

Colossians 3:24 says, *"…since you know that you will receive an inheritance from the Lord as a reward. It is the Lord Christ you are serving."*

Observation. It's important to truly understand and be fully committed to doing everything for the glory of the Lord Jesus, even in your daily work. The rewards for working with honesty, integrity, and respect will yield plenty in heaven. When things just don't seem to be going the right way, remember that there will come a morning when you'll stand in the presence of Jesus. Then the rewards will be incredible!

You are serving Jesus, and that's all that should matter. Believe me, I know this is easy to say, but it takes a lifetime to fully understand.

John MacArthur said,

> God's credits and rewards will be appropriate to the attitude and action of our work. No good thing done for his glory will go unrewarded… The Lord ensures the believer that he will receive a just, eternal compensation for his efforts, even if his earthly boss or master does not compensate fairly. God deals with obedience and disobedience impartially. Christians are not to presume on their faith in order to justify disobedience to an authority or employer.[133]

Revelation 20:12 affirms this when it says,

> And I saw the dead, great and small, standing before the throne, and books were opened. Another book was opened, which is the book of life. The dead were judged according to what they had done as recorded in the books.

It's not up to us to take matters into our own hands. We do our work as unto the Lord and let Him handle any injustices.

As Colossians 3:24 reminds us, *"It is the Lord Christ you are serving."* Imagine that the Lord was sitting in the office beside you. Think of your workstation, your area, or your locker, with your photographs and sayings on the wall… would you remove anything? Think of the conversations you have with other employees or peers… would your speech change? Think of the way you respond to your supervisor when they give you an assignment… would you change your attitude? Would Jesus describe you as working wholeheartedly or just putting in time? Would you resemble someone who works for the Lord and gives glory to Him, or would there be anything to glorify?

As you can see, we bear a tremendous responsibility when we're labelled as Christians in the workplace. I once heard someone say, "If you were in a court of law charged with being a Christian, would there be enough evidence to prove you guilty?" Put the Lord Jesus in charge of your life and make sure you want Him as your audience, and Him alone.

God said in Hebrews 13:5–6, *"'Never will I leave you; never will I forsake you.' So we say with confidence, 'The Lord is my helper; I will not be afraid. What can mere mortals do to me?'"*

I want to conclude this section with a great Old Testament verse that speaks in the context of a home but could certainly be applied to your career. It's something Joshua wrote as his life was drawing to a close:

> *Now fear the Lord and serve him with all faithfulness. Throw away the gods your ancestors worshiped beyond the Euphrates River and in Egypt, and serve the Lord. But if serving the Lord seems undesirable to you, then choose for yourselves this day whom you will serve, whether the gods your ancestors served beyond the Euphrates, or the gods of the Amorites, in whose land you are living. But as for me and my household, we will serve the Lord.*
>
> —Joshua 24:14–15

What a great finish that is, what a crescendo: "We will serve the Lord." Imagine the booming drums, the song rising to a fever pitch. This verse is loaded with practical applications that are as relevant today as when it was written thousands of years ago.

Ephesians 6:5–8 also sums up this passage:

> *Slaves, obey your earthly masters with respect and fear, and with sincerity of heart, just as you would obey Christ. Obey them not only to win their favor when their eye is on you, but as slaves of Christ, doing the will of God from your heart. Serve wholeheartedly, as if you were serving the Lord, not people, because you know that the Lord will reward each one for whatever good they do, whether they are slave or free.*

We serve Jesus Christ, a risen Saviour!

Application. Here are three ways you can apply this truth to your life:

1. Live knowing that your reward will come from heaven. What a day that will be!
2. Serve the Lord not only on Sunday but while you're working.
3. Have a mentality that shouts, "I will serve the Lord!"

It's time to see what the Bible has to say regarding those in management. This is all about how you treat those over whom you have been given responsibility. This is just one verse, but it holds so much meaning that it can take a long time to fully grasp.

Colossians 4:1 says, "*Masters, provide your slaves with what is right and fair, because you know that you also have a Master in heaven.*"

Observation. This is a verse that anyone in any type of management or oversight role should not only read, but burn into their memory.

When I became a regional manager at the age of twenty-eight, I wasn't aware of anyone else in the industry who had risen to management so young. Only a year and a half earlier, I had been sitting at an order desk handling customer service. Unfortunately for me, this success often went to my head and I held myself in very high regard. This almost proved disastrous, and during this period I learned some really difficult lessons.

Galatians 6:7–8 talks about sowing and repeating:

Do not be deceived: God cannot be mocked. A man reaps what he sows. Whoever sows to please their flesh, from the flesh will reap destruction; whoever sows to please the Spirit, from the Spirit will reap eternal life.

This passage has three parts to it. The first discusses what you are doing to God, the second lists the negative results of this, and the third lists the positive results. Volumes could be written about these verses.

I eventually learned that if you treat your staff in a fair, honest, and righteous manner, most people will work very hard. I say *most* because over the course of my career there were people who didn't do a good job and their issues had to be addressed. I say this so that you understand that being in a management position does require you to do the right thing for your company, church, or organization.

Overall, I realized that there were not that many bad employees, but a lot of bad managers—of which I was one. I knew things had to change.

I implore companies to spend time training managers, and this verse alone could change the way a person treats their staff. For many years, I attended training seminars, read books authored by successful people, attended college business courses, and listened to motivational speakers. Most importantly, I studied my Bible and attempted to apply what I learned.

I had a game-changing experience when I attended a seminar featuring speaker Zig Ziglar, whom I later found out was a Christian. This man is among the greatest storytellers and motivational speakers I've ever heard. I would strongly recommend you go online and listen to some of his messages. They're incredible and were just what I needed at that time in my career.

The game-changing comment is one I've tried to live by for the rest of my career, not only in business but life in general. Zig said, "You can have anything in life you want, if you help enough other people get what they want." This immediately caused me to look at my staff in a different way.

My approach to management changed from that day forward. When dealing with people I worked with, I looked at more than just their work;

I got to know the person and tried to better understand their goals and dreams. It wasn't all about me!

Once I took an interest in their lives and jointly assisted them in reaching their goals and dreams, a funny thing happened: our business started to grow, and we had a very motivated group of people. This was right and fair, just as the verse states.

Honestly, I never expected things to go so well.

In Philippians 2:3–4, you'll find a great passage that could serve as your personal goal: *"Do nothing out of selfish ambition or vain conceit. Rather, in humility value others above yourselves, not looking to your own interests but each of you to the interests of the others."* This is called servant leadership, and when it's carried out in a godly manner it will reap great rewards—and most importantly, it will honour the Lord Jesus Christ.

John MacArthur states this so well in his commentary on Ephesians 6:9:

> There should be mutual honour and respect from Christian employers to their employees, based on their common allegiance to the Lord. The Spirit-filled boss uses his authority and power with justice and grace—never putting people under threats, never abusive or inconsiderate. He realizes that he has a heavenly Master who is impartial.[134]

William MacDonald adds the closing comments of his commentary on the same verse: "Earthly distinctions are leveled in the presence of the Lord. Both Master/Manager and Servant/Employee will one day give an account to Him."[135]

Application. Here are three ways to apply this verse to your life:

1. Treat your staff in a manner that is right and fair, as the Lord will judge you one day.
2. Help others to achieve their dreams and goals.
3. Mutually respect one another.

Colossians 4:2 says, "*Devote yourselves to prayer, being watchful and thankful.*" The last part of this verse states the key to success in business and life: be thankful.

Being a Christian isn't easy in this world, as our thinking is completely opposite to the world's views. Thankfulness is also contrary to the ways of the world. In a world where everyone feels they're owed a living—and most feel a sense of entitlement—thankfulness rarely plays a role. But thankfulness is the way in which God wants us to live. These two small words—be thankful—play an enormous role in our walk with Jesus Christ.

Observation. If there's any area of my life that I've been relatively consistent in, it's maintaining a spirit of thankfulness. Even though I was a vice president for almost twenty-five years, I would still walk into my office in the morning and stand in disbelief that the Lord had provided me with so much in my career. Never had I dreamed that my career would take off the way it did and continue for many years.

To have a thankful heart is a wonderful gift from God and it truly opens up an attitude of gratitude in your life. There are three wonderful character traits that every Christian hopefully strives to embody, and they're summed up in these three verses:

> *Let the peace of Christ rule in your hearts, since as members of one body you were called to peace. And be thankful. Let the message of Christ dwell among you richly as you teach and admonish one another with all wisdom through psalms, hymns, and songs from the Spirit, singing to God with gratitude in your hearts. And whatever you do, whether in word or deed, do it all in the name of the Lord Jesus, giving thanks to God the Father through him.*
> —Colossians 3:15–17

Thankfulness is paramount in every verse of this passage. This is the way God wants us to live, as it is an incredible way to honour and glorify our Lord Jesus Christ.

Another great verse for thankfulness is Philippians 4:6, which says, "*Do not be anxious about anything, but in every situation, by prayer and petition, with thanksgiving, present your requests to God."* William MacDonald has summarized this verse as saying that we should be "anxious for nothing, prayerful in everything, thankful for anything."[136]

Also, I thank God daily for my salvation in Jesus. There is no greater truth to be thankful for in this life than having Jesus as my Lord and Saviour. How can we not have a thankful heart when we know for certain that our names are written in heaven and we will one day see the One who died for us?

Application. You can apply this verse in two ways:

1. Be a thankful person.
2. Praise Jesus daily for all He has done for you.

When I asked Paul where he was when he wrote these messages about careers (Colossians 3:22–4:2), he told me that he was in prison. How is that possible? Only with love for Jesus and the leading of the Holy Spirit could Paul write such truths under those circumstances.

Paul offers us a roadmap for business, and when implemented in our day-to-day lives, work, family, and life will improve and we will live for Jesus. People may dislike you, even to the point of hatred, but if you work the way Paul describes in this passage, they will never be able to condemn your work habits or ethics. Remember, be thankful!

- Chapter Eleven -

Rocky III and the Bible

This is going to be an unusual chapter, as I make connections between the Bible and a film that has profoundly influenced my life and walk with the Lord. My hope is to show you biblical truths that I have picked up from the movie *Rocky III*.[137]

Let's begin with Proverbs 24:16, which tells us that *"for though the righteous fall seven times, they rise again, but the wicked stumble when calamity strikes."* If that doesn't describe Rocky, I'm not sure what it does.

You may be asking, "How can you equate a movie about boxing to the Bible?" Here's my answer: in the same way that the character of Rocky is spurred to action and endurance, I have found many verses in the Bible that motivate and encourage people to action as well. In the Bible, there are some very positive books and chapters, although most people think it just contains lists of things you can't do, along with judgement, hell, and damnation. These are all part of the Bible, but there are many wise communications regarding living a happy and positive life, and even how to pick yourself up when you've been knocked down—just like with Rocky.

Let me first explain the important influence that *Rocky III* had on my life. I had seen both *Rocky* and *Rocky II*; both tell great stories of someone who's down and out and fights back to become a champion. They were inspiring movies. But *Rocky III?* now that was an epic movie!

The day my son was born, I left the hospital with my wife and new son looking forward to some peace and recovery. When I arrived home, my brother came over to visit. My wife and I were exhausted that evening, as the day had started bright and early at 4:30 a.m.

During the visit, my brother asked me what I thought of *Rocky III*. I told him I hadn't seen it and he almost fell off his chair.

"You haven't seen *Rocky III?*" he said. "We have to go now!"

Before I knew what was happening, we were in his car on the way to a theatre in downtown Toronto. This was the 10:00 p.m. show on a Thursday night, and the huge theatre was packed. It was noisy while we waited for the film to begin.

The lights dimmed and the theatre went quiet. Out of nowhere, my brother stood up and started chanting, "Rocky! Rocky!" The entire theatre then erupted in the chant. My brother did stuff like this all the time; there was never a dull moment when you were with him.

The movie began with a history of all the wins Rocky had accumulated so far. When he began his career, he'd focused on nothing but his profession; to be a champion boxer meant you had to be mean and nasty in the ring, which he exuded in abundance.

But after defending his title ten times, he started to do a very dangerous thing: he began to not only read, but he started to believe the press clippings that were coming out about him. It's one thing to make it to the top, but it's another to stay on top. Endorsements came flowing in for Rocky, along with newfound wealth. He no longer had to fight just to pay the rent. His life was on cruise control. However, he had lost his edge and thought he had it all.

The following scriptures come to mind:

> *So, if you think you are standing firm, be careful that you don't fall! No temptation has overtaken you except what is common to mankind. And God is faithful; he will not let you be tempted beyond what you can bear. But when you are tempted, he will also provide a way out so that you can endure it.*
> —1 Corinthians 10:12–13

Let's start with 1 Corinthians 10:12, which says, "*So, if you think you are standing firm, be careful that you don't fall!*"

Observation. The apostle Paul explained that this is a trap many people fall into as their lives become more successful. They begin to feel a false sense of security and think they no longer need God. This verse is truly a wake-up call to show that life without God, no matter how successful it seems, is ultimately worthless.

Peter had a similar experience, as outlined in Luke 22:33–34:

> *Peter said to him, "Lord, I am ready to go with you both to prison and to death." Jesus said, "I tell you, Peter, the rooster will not crow this day, until you deny three times that you know me."* (ESV)

Then Luke 22:54–62 adds,

> *Then they seized him [Jesus] and led him away, bringing him into the high priest's house, and Peter was following at a distance. And when they had kindled a fire in the middle of the courtyard and sat down together, Peter sat down among them. Then a servant girl, seeing him as he sat in the light and looking closely at him, said, "This man also was with him." But he denied it, saying, "Woman, I do not know him." And a little later someone else saw him and said, "You also are one of them." But Peter said, "Man, I am not." And after an interval of about an hour still another insisted, saying, "Certainly this man also was with him, for he too is a Galilean." But Peter said, "Man, I do not know what you are talking about." And immediately, while he was still speaking, the rooster crowed. And the Lord turned and looked at Peter. And Peter remembered the saying of the Lord, how he had said to him, "Before the rooster crows today, you will deny me three times." And he went out and wept bitterly.* (ESV)

Thankfully, similarly to Rocky, this isn't where the story ends for Peter. He goes on to start the church and is used in a mighty way for Jesus for the rest of his life, going so far as to die for his faith.

Let's move forward into Revelation to discuss what happens when your goal is nothing but material wealth. Jesus issues this rebuke: *"You say, 'I am rich; I have acquired wealth and do not need a thing.' But you do not realize that you are wretched, pitiful, poor, blind and naked"* (Revelation

3:17). Now, that's quite a statement—especially when your security is found in money.

William MacDonald writes,

> They constitute a warning to self-confidence: Let him who thinks he stands firm take heed lest he falls. Perhaps this refers especially to the strong believer who thinks he can dabble with self-gratification and not be affected by it. Such a person is in greatest danger of falling under the disciplinary hand of God.[138]

Keep in mind that Satan and his demons are out there, ready to pounce.

Application. Here are three applications for your daily life:

1. Don't get too cocky or overconfident. Put your hope in the Lord Jesus.
2. Be obedient through prayer and the study of God's Word.
3. Do nothing out of selfish ambition.

One of the innumerable great things about the Bible is what I call "the next verse" principle. Isn't it great to know that when you read a verse like 1 Corinthians 10:12, which offers such a stinging rebuke, you can turn to the next verse and read about great hope? There's no way to stop at such a challenging verse and not tell the rest of the story.

Let's take another look at 1 Corinthians 10:13:

> *No temptation has overtaken you except what is common to mankind. And God is faithful; he will not let you be tempted beyond what you can bear. But when you are tempted, he will also provide a way out so that you can endure it.*

Observation. All of us will be tempted. That's nothing new. But we need to praise God, as He is faithful. 1 Corinthians 1:9 says, *"God is faithful, who has called you into fellowship with his Son, Jesus Christ our Lord."*

William MacDonald makes this comment about 1 Corinthians 10:13:

But then Paul adds a marvelous word of encouragement for those who are tempted. He teaches that the testing, trials, and temptations which face us are common to all. However, God is faithful; he will not let you be tempted beyond what you can bear. He does not promise to deliver us from temptation or testing, but He does promise to limit its intensity…

Paul would comfort them with the thought that God would not allow any unbearable temptation to come their way. At the same time, they should be warned that they should not expose themselves to temptation.[139]

It should also be noted that the text says *when* you are tempted, not *if*. God will provide a way out, not me! Whenever I handle things on my own, using my own power and ability, I lose. God, however, can get me through anything!

Without God, I am nothing. How incredible it is to realize that the Creator of the universe will help me. Praise God!

Application. Here are three ways to apply this verse:

1. Stay away from areas or places of temptation.
2. When temptations come, quickly lean on Jesus and the Word of God.
3. When undergoing temptations, look for God's escape route.

While Rocky thought he had it all and nothing to worry about, another boxer named Clubber Lang made his way up through the ranks of the heavyweight division. He was mean and nasty, but more importantly, he was hungry for the championship. Nothing in the world was more important to him than becoming the heavyweight champion of the world, meaning that Rocky would eventually have to face him.

When this man first appeared in the movie, played by Mr. T, his head covering the entire theatre screen with his mohawk haircut, I have to admit I was scared!

In addition to this, just before the fight between them was to begin, Rocky's mentor and manager had a heart attack while entering the arena.

Rocky III and the Bible

Rocky had to go to the ring without his manager and support system—not the ideal conditions to begin the fight of his life.

When Rocky finally met Clubber in the ring, he was pummelled and destroyed, and right after the fight his manager died in his arms. After these devastating losses, Rocky went into a dark place of not wanting to do anything, let alone fight again. It's what he did in this place of desperation that I found so incredibly motivating, helping me through tough times even to this day. As the film continues, we hear the song "Eye of the Tiger," which becomes an anthem to never give up, never lose your edge, and fight to the end.

In many ways, this presents a description of the Christian life. The difference is that my dependence rests on Jesus rather than myself. Rocky was an inspiration to many, encouraging them to stay motivated and not give up. Many verses in God's Word are similarly positive and encouraging. My hope is to show you some great verses that will motivate you and enable you to glorify God in the process.

Paul was a great example of a motivated man. Honestly, he could have been a motivational speaker. He wrote Philippians 4, which is one of the most positive chapters in the Bible and was one of the first passages of Scripture I memorized. It has some of the most uplifting language you'll encounter anywhere—and the most amazing part of this passage is the fact that Paul wrote it while in prison.

As we journey through Philippians 4:4–9, I hope you'll hear the Rocky theme song, "Gonna Fly Now," playing in the background.

Philippians 4:4–9 says,

> *Rejoice in the Lord always. I will say it again: Rejoice! Let your gentleness be evident to all. The Lord is near. Do not be anxious about anything, but in every situation, by prayer and petition, with thanksgiving, present your requests to God. And the peace of God, which transcends all understanding, will guard your hearts and your minds in Christ Jesus.*
>
> *Finally, brothers and sisters, whatever is true, whatever is noble, whatever is right, whatever is pure, whatever is lovely, whatever is admirable—if anything is excellent or praiseworthy—think*

about such things. Whatever you have learned or received or heard from me, or seen in me—put it into practice. And the God of peace will be with you.

Let's start with Philippians 4:4, which simply says, "*Rejoice in the Lord always. I will say it again: Rejoice!*"

Observation. If there is one attribute we should constantly embody as Christians, it is joy. It should be a constant state of mind, resting deep in our DNA. We can live in the knowledge that we cannot lose; even death has lost its victory over us, as we will be with the Lord forever. That's the reason Paul repeats it and says it again: "Rejoice!"

Can you imagine what the world would be like if all Christians were known as people who rejoice? I'm not sure that is the image we portray to others, but it is what God wants us to do.

In the book of Luke, the Lord Jesus gives us a true reason to rejoice:

The seventy-two returned with joy and said, "Lord, even the demons submit to us in your name."

He replied, "I saw Satan fall like lightning from heaven. I have given you authority to trample on snakes and scorpions and to overcome all the power of the enemy; nothing will harm you. However, do not rejoice that the spirits submit to you, but rejoice that your names are written in heaven."

—Luke 10:17–20

Wow! Now that is reason to rejoice. Can you imagine being present to hear that statement? This was the most incredible experience those men ever had, and then Jesus said, "That's nothing. You are heaven-bound!" Rejoice in the Lord always, and I will say it again: Rejoice!

Application. Here are two applications for your daily life:

1. Live a life of joy as you rejoice in the Lord.
2. Rejoice, because your name is written in heaven.

Philippians 4:5 says, "*Let your gentleness be evident to all. The Lord is near.*" In the Amplified Bible, we read it this way: "*Let all men know and perceive and recognize your unselfishness (your considerateness, your forbearing spirit). The Lord is near [He is coming soon]*" (AMPC).

Observation. In the English Standard Version, we see the word "reasonableness." John MacArthur comments on the use of this word:

> This refers to contentment with and generosity toward others. It can also refer to mercy or leniency toward the faults and failures of others. It can even refer to patience in someone who submits to injustice or mistreatment without retaliating. Graciousness with humility encompasses all of the above.[140]

While reading MacArthur's commentary, I was struck by the thought that this is a lifelong venture. This verse alone could take a lifetime to understand and apply. If a person could just live this verse, their entire life would change dramatically.

As I read this, I am thankful for Philippians 1:6, which says, "*[B]eing confident of this, that he who began a good work in you will carry it on to completion until the day of Christ Jesus.*" The Bible is full of great principles to live by, and they can only be achieved with the help of the Holy Spirit directing our lives.

Let's move forward to the next phrase, which tells us that "*the Lord is near.*" Several other scriptures reinforce this statement:

Yet you are near, Lord, and all your commands are true.
—Psalm 119:151

The Lord is near to all who call on him, to all who call on him in truth.
—Psalm 145:18

In just a little while, he who is coming will come and will not delay.
—Hebrews 10:37

> *Be patient, then, brothers and sisters, until the Lord's coming. See how the farmer waits for the land to yield its valuable crop, patiently waiting for the autumn and spring rains. You too, be patient and stand firm, because the Lord's coming is near.*
> —James 5:7–8

Knowing this should have a significant impact on our lives. When He returns, will He find us doing His will as the His prayer says? *"[Y]our will be done, on earth as it is in heaven"* (Matthew 6:10). Or will He find us not doing His will? We should live a life that honours Him and make sure we are ready for His return.

Application. This verse can be applied in three ways today:

1. Live a life with the expectation that the Lord could return at any time.
2. Be a reasonable, gentle person.
3. Persevere to live this verse daily in your life.

Philippians 4:6 says, *"Do not be anxious about anything, but in every situation, by prayer and petition, with thanksgiving, present your requests to God."*

Observation. What a statement this is: *"Do not be anxious about anything."* Is anxiety an issue for people? *The World's Bible Dictionary* tells us,

> Anxiety; In a world where people face daily troubles and future uncertainties, it is natural that often they become anxious. Those who trust in God, however, need not be burdened by anxiety. God understands their troubles and concerns, and he promises them His peace if they cast their cares on Him. Jesus reassures Christians with the promise that since God gives them life, he can also give them whatever is necessary to maintain life. God is a loving Father who knows how to care for his children. To refuse to trust Him is to act like those who do not know Him. In fact, people's anxiety concerning the affairs of life is often what prevents them from coming to know God. They refuse to give serious attention to the one thing that can

save them from anxiety, namely, the gospel of Jesus Christ. On the other hand, when people put God first by allowing Him to reign in their lives, they find that He is able to relieve them of life's natural anxieties.[141]

Jesus sums up this verse in the Sermon on the Mount:

Therefore I tell you, do not be anxious about your life, what you will eat or what you will drink, nor about your body, what you will put on. Is not life more than food, and the body more than clothing? Look at the birds of the air: they neither sow nor reap nor gather into barns, and yet your heavenly Father feeds them. Are you not of more value than they? And which of you by being anxious can add a single hour to his span of life? And why are you anxious about clothing? Consider the lilies of the field, how they grow: they neither toil nor spin, yet I tell you, even Solomon in all his glory was not arrayed like one of these. But if God so clothes the grass of the field, which today is alive and tomorrow is thrown into the oven, will he not much more clothe you, O you of little faith? Therefore do not be anxious, saying, "What shall we eat?" or "What shall we drink?" or "What shall we wear?" For the Gentiles seek after all these things, and your heavenly Father knows that you need them all. But seek first the kingdom of God and his righteousness, and all these things will be added to you.

Therefore do not be anxious about tomorrow, for tomorrow will be anxious for itself. Sufficient for the day is its own trouble.
—Matthew 6:25–34, ESV

The key verse in this passage, the one worth repeating, comes from Matthew 6:33: *"But seek first his kingdom and his righteousness, and all these things will be given to you as well."*

Chuck Swindoll commented on this verse:

When the temptation to worry first comes, that is the critical moment. Our tendency is to entertain it. We let [it] in onto the front porch and are hospitable because it has visited us so many times. We get it a drink of water and let it rest up–before we know it, worry has made itself home in our lives again. Our tendency to let worry in must be stopped! Worry comes and says, "You'd better not overlook this possibility. Or that one." That's when we need to say, "No! I'm going to commit this worry to God right now. I refuse to entertain it, even on the porch of my life. I'm going to seek God's Kingdom about all else and trust Him in everything."[142]

John MacArthur adds, "Fret and worry indicate a lack of trust in God's wisdom, sovereignty, or power. Delighting in the Lord and meditating on his word are a great antidote to anxiety."[143]

Okay. So all that is great, but what do we do with this? I'm glad you asked! Let's move on to the rest of Philippians 4:6, specifically the part that tells us to *"in every situation, by prayer and petition, with thanksgiving, present your requests to God."*

William MacDonald wrote,

> Is it really possible for a Christian to be anxious for nothing? It is possible as long as we have the resource of believing prayer. The rest of the verse goes on to explain how our lives can be free from sinful fretting. Everything should be taken to the Lord in prayer. Everything means everything. There is nothing too great or small for his loving care! Prayer is both an act and an atmosphere. We come to the Lord at specific times and bring specific requests before Him. But it is also possible to live in an atmosphere of prayer. It is possible that the mood of our life should be a prayerful mood. Perhaps the word prayer in this verse signifies the overall attitude of our life, whereas supplication signifies the specific requests which we bring to the Lord. But then we should notice that our requests should be made know to God with thanksgiving. Someone has summarized this verse by saying that we should be "anxious for nothing, prayerful in everything, thankful for anything."[144]

As I look through this great commentary by MacDonald, one thing hit me: the importance of being thankful. I've said it before and will say it again: our names are written in heaven! What more could we possibly need than the assurance of spending eternity in heaven with our Lord and Saviour Jesus Christ?

My prayer is that as Christians we will be known as thankful people. Knowing that we've been forgiven for our sins, that the Lord Jesus paid our debt in full, should truly make us scream "Hallelujah!" and be extremely grateful. What an incredible gift from God! May I never lose sight of this wonderful, life-changing event in my life and thank God daily for His Son Jesus.

John MacArthur adds, "All difficulties are within God's purposes. Gratitude to God accompanies all true prayer."[145]

When I think of this verse and how powerful it is, I am reminded of a hymn that speaks to the point Paul is trying to get across to his readers. The hymn is "What a Friend We Have In Jesus":

What a friend we have in Jesus, all our sins and griefs to bear!
What a privilege to carry everything to God in prayer!
O what peace we often forfeit, O what needless pain we bear,
all because we do not carry everything to God in prayer!

Have we trials and temptations? Is there trouble anywhere?
We should never be discouraged; take it to the Lord in prayer!
Can we find a friend so faithful who will all our sorrows share?
Jesus knows our every weakness; take it to the Lord in prayer!

Are we weak and heavy laden, cumbered with a load of care?
Precious Savior, still our refuge—take it to the Lord in prayer!
Do your friends despise, forsake you? Take it to the Lord in prayer!
In his arms he'll take and shield you; you will find a solace there.[146]

Application. Here are four ways to apply this verse to your life:

1. Take everything to God in prayer before anxiety comes.
2. Keep yourself in a constant atmosphere or mood of prayer.
3. Have a specific time of daily prayer and list your requests of God, and write down His answers.
4. Be thankful.

Philippians 4:7 says, *"And the peace of God, which transcends all understanding, will guard your hearts and your minds in Christ Jesus."*

Observation. The peace of God is like no other peace since it's supernatural and transcends all understanding. This is a peace the secular world and non-believers will never understand. Only those in the family of God will be able to share in God's peace.

On November 22, 1873, while crossing the Atlantic on the steamship *Ville du Havre*, the vessel carrying Horatio Spafford's family was struck by an iron sailing ship. Two hundred and twenty-six people lost their lives, as the *Ville du Havre* sank in just twelve minutes. All four of Horatio's daughters perished.

Remarkably, his wife Anna survived the tragedy. Those rescued, including Anna—who was found unconscious, floating on a plank of wood—subsequently arrived in Cardiff, South Wales. There, Anna immediately sent a telegram to her husband, which included the words "Saved alone…"

Receiving Anna's message, Horatio set off at once to be reunited with his wife. One particular day, during the voyage, the captain summoned him to the bridge of the vessel. Pointing to his charts, he explained that they were passing over the very spot where the *Ville du Havre* had sunk, and where his daughters had died.

It is said that Spafford then returned to his cabin and wrote the hymn "It Is Well with My Soul," penning the opening line, "When peace like a river, attendeth my way…" Other accounts say it was written at a later date, but obviously the voyage was one of deep pathos, and it was the clear inspiration for this moving and well-loved hymn.

Horatio's faith in God never faltered. The song he wrote is an incredible testimony to God's peace:

> When peace like a river attendeth my way,
> when sorrows like sea billows roll;
> whatever my lot, thou hast taught me to say,
> "It is well, it is well with my soul."
> It is well with my soul;
> it is well, it is well with my soul.
>
> Though Satan should buffet, though trials should come,
> let this blest assurance control:
> that Christ has regarded my helpless estate,
> and has shed his own blood for my soul.
>
> My sin oh, the bliss of this glorious thought!
> my sin, not in part, but the whole,
> is nailed to the cross, and I bear it no more;
> praise the Lord, praise the Lord, O my soul!
>
> O Lord, haste the day when my faith shall be sight,
> the clouds be rolled back as a scroll;
> the trump shall resound and the Lord shall descend;
> even so, it is well with my soul.[147]

Add to this amazing hymn the words of Jesus's promise in John 14:27: *"Peace I leave you; my peace I give you. I do not give to you as the world gives. Do not let your hearts be troubled and do not be afraid."* This is the only kind of peace that could make Horatio Spafford have the faith in the Lord and trust to write such a hymn.

The Old Testament contains another great verse on peace: *"You will keep in perfect peace those whose minds are steadfast, because they trust in you"* (Isaiah 26:3). Warren Wiersbe comments,

> The peace of God stands over the two areas that create worry—the heart (wrong feelings) and the mind (wrong thinking). When we give our hearts to Christ in salvation, we experience "peace with God," but the "peace of God," takes us a step farther

into His blessings. This does not mean the absence of trials on the outside, but it does mean a quiet confidence within, regardless of circumstances, people, or things.[148]

Let's not forget the role model of this peace, Daniel, who, when ordered not to pray to anyone but the king of the land, prayed anyway and was sentenced to death in a lion's den. Daniel was able to spend the night with lions in perfect peace while the king tossed and turned, unable to sleep. This not only transcends but defies all worldly understanding of how things should work.

Regarding peace and transcending all understanding, John MacArthur wrote,

> Inner calm or tranquility is promised to the believer who has a thankful attitude based on unwavering confidence that God is able and willing to do what is best for his children. Transcends all understanding refers to the divine origin of peace. It transcends human intellect, analysis and insight.[149]

What I would give to have that kind of peace! We see in these examples that, with the help of the Holy Spirit, this peace will grow every day. God is in control and every day your faith will grow as God continues to prove Himself over and over, and as you study and apply His Word.

Philippians 4:7 also says that the peace of God *"will guard your hearts and minds in Christ Jesus."* Only the peace of Jesus can sustain us through the storms of life. But the key to this phrase is that we must *guard* it.

Amy Watson, of Statista.com, sums up the situation this way:

> The average weekly time spent watching television in Canada in the 2019/20 broadcast year was 25 hours a week among adults aged 18 or above, and those over the age of 55 watched the most television per week at 38.5 hours. Meanwhile, teens watched just over 12 hours each week.[150]

Personally, I love to watch TV. But if we aren't careful, it can take over our thoughts and minds. Also, consider the way the media presents cable news—they're trying to move you in the direction of their thoughts. Honestly, I rarely believe anything that is presented by the news media.

Let's also talk about social media, such as Facebook, YouTube, Instagram, Twitter, Snapchat, and TikTok. When we factor in all these mediums of communication, it's easy to see how we can be driven in whatever direction the latest quote of the day sends us. Just so you can understand the magnitude of this, that's around three and a half billion people worldwide.

Today, most people's eyes are focused on their phones, and nothing interferes with that. Someone can be in a face-to-face conversation, but when they hear the *ting* of their phone's notification, they'll stop talking to you to check to see what's happening.

I enjoy social media, but there's a huge risk of letting down your mental guard.

So, where is Jesus or one's belief in God in the midst of all this? It has to compete against approximately six hours per day of television and social media, plus going to work—not to mention the time spent bringing up a family, looking after a home, and of course sleeping.

This is what I mean when I say that we have to guard our hearts and minds.

If living for Jesus isn't the number one priority in your life, you can be swept away by all the distractions of the world, which leads to a very destructive end. In today's age, we don't seem to even give it a second thought.

My hope is to lead you to the Scriptures and learn what the Christian life is all about, understanding how it can bring you the kind of joy that none of the above will ever give you. So be on your guard, because your life depends on it.

In some cases, people combat this problem by attending church on Sundays and hoping it will get them through the week. Let's do the math: one hour on Sunday versus forty-two hours per week of television and social media. I'm not saying you shouldn't watch television or participate in social media; what I'm saying is that this should not dominate your life, because it will never help you find the joy of Jesus or the peace of God.

My prayer is that God's Word will come alive to you and that prayer will become a daily staple in your life. If not, you aren't guarding your heart and mind in Christ Jesus.

John MacArthur sums this up rather well:

> Paul was not making a distinction between the two (heart and mind), he was giving a comprehensive statement referring to the whole inner person. Because of the believer's union with Christ, he guards his inner being with his peace.[151]

Application. Here are three ways to apply this verse today:

1. Seek peace daily by deciding to make Jesus the number one priority in your life.
2. Guard your heart and mind through spending daily time in prayer and studying the Bible.
3. Dial back the amount of time you spend on television and social media and turn it over to the Lord.

As we move into Philippians 4:8, you'll see some of the most uplifting and motivating words found anywhere in Scripture. After all the ways Paul has told us to find peace and rid ourselves of anxiety, he starts this next verse with the word *finally*, which tells us to expect that we're approaching the ultimate takeaway from this section of Scripture.

It will be motivating to take this next verse one word at a time. If you can live by these eight words alone—true, noble, right, pure, lovely, admirable, excellent, and praiseworthy—your life will change dramatically. These are words to live by, and the words of Philippians 4:8 are the words that I want my life to mirror.

Chuck Swindoll's commentary of Philippians 4:8 begins this way:

> Do you have occasional idle moments during the day? We all do, of course. In those pauses, what do you let your mind dwell on? What do you think about when you don't have to think about

anything in particular? It can be easy to ruminate on thoughts of blame or self-pity. Take Philippians 4:8 to heart![152]

William MacDonald's commentary regarding this verse says,

> Now the apostle gives a closing bit of advice concerning the thought life. The Bible everywhere teaches that we can control what we think. It is useless to develop a defeatist attitude, saying that we simply cannot help it when our minds are filled with unwelcome thoughts. The fact of the matter is that we can help it. The secret lies in positive thinking. It is a well-known principle—the expulsive power of a new affection. A person cannot entertain evil thoughts and thoughts about the Lord Jesus at the same time. If then, an evil thought should come to him, he should immediately get rid of it by meditating on the Person and work of Christ. The more enlightened psychologists and psychiatrists of the day have come to agree with the Apostle Paul on this matter. They stress the dangers of negative thinking.[153]

I love the way The Message translation states this verse:

> *Summing it all up, friends, I'd say you'll do best by filling your minds and meditating on things true, noble, reputable, authentic, compelling, gracious—the best, not the worst; the beautiful, not the ugly; things to praise, not things to curse.*
> —Philippians 4:8, MSG

Are you hearing the Rocky theme again in the background of your mind? This verse could change your life for the better and improve your thought process in ways you would never dream of.

Now, let's examine each phase of this verse and watch how it grows to a crescendo at the end: *"Finally, brothers and sisters, whatever is true, whatever is noble, whatever is right, whatever is pure, whatever is lovely, whatever is admirable—if anything is excellent or praiseworthy—think about such things"* (Philippians 4:8).

The word "whatever" is used at the start of each of the middle six phrases. It is a version of "whatsoever," which is "used as an intensifier with indefinite pronouns and determines such as none, anybody, etc.," according to *Collins English Dictionary*.[154] I love the word "intensifier" in that definition, because that's exactly what it is. The Bible is plainly saying that this is what you should be thinking about in your daily walk of life.

Let's start with the phrase *"whatever is true."*

Observation. The word "true" is defined by *Collins English Dictionary* as follows: "not false, fictional or illusory; factual; conforming with reality. Real, not synthetic. Faithful and loyal."[155] Well, you don't hear the word "illusory" every day, so I looked up synonyms for that word and was surprised at what I discovered: "misleading, unreal, deceptive, false and erroneous."[156]

Chuck Swindoll says,

> The cynic will rush to criticize ideas of this mindset. "This is living in unreality. It's a dreamworld philosophy." But give some thought to the six things Paul says we should set our minds on. Note that the apostle's first descriptive word is true. That is, Paul urges us to think about things that are reliable, valid, and honest, not deceptive or illusory.[157] It is not a dreamworld. Christ introduces us to the real world, where He is in control. A dreamworld in contrast, is an imaginary one where the person is his or her own maker.[158]

What is your truth today? Where do you go to find out what's right and wrong? Do you think the news media or social media always tells the truth? People depend on these avenues of communication for information to help them live their lives. It amazes me how many people won't start their day until they read what their horoscope has advised. I have a tendency not to go to the stars for direction, but the One who made the stars.

We must not stop with simply *knowing* what's true; we must also *tell* the truth. I once heard someone say that telling the truth takes a deliberate effort. Now that's the truth! You should be known as a person of truth and your word should be your bond. Unfortunately, that's usually not the case today.

Also, you shouldn't have to make any grandiose comments prior to telling the truth, such as saying "Honest to God…" And just as a side note, that comment breaks the third commandment not to take the name of the Lord in vain. Jesus put it so eloquently, and yet so simply, in Matthew 5:37: *"All you need to say is simply 'Yes' or 'No'; anything beyond this comes from the evil one."*

Since I mentioned the third commandment, I should also add the ninth commandment, which says, *"You shall not give false testimony…"* (Exodus 20:16) When someone is about to testify in a court of law, the bailiff asks, "Do you swear to tell the truth, the whole truth, and nothing but the truth?" Before everything having to do with God was taken out of the legal process, the witness was asked to hold a Bible in their hand and repeat, "I swear by Almighty God that the evidence I shall give to the courts in this case shall be the truth, the whole truth, and nothing but the truth." For a Christian, it should be a given that you will tell the truth.

We need truth, and the only place to find it is in God's Word and through the saving faith of Jesus.

So what does the Bible say about the truth? This brought me back to a discussion I had with John the apostle, who told me that truth brings with it a sense of freedom. As a matter of fact, it is one of the only ways a person can be truly free.

John reminded me of what Jesus said in John 8:31–32: *"If you hold to my teaching, you are really my disciples. Then you will know the truth, and the truth will set you free."* Further along, Jesus continued, *"So if the Son sets you free, you will be free indeed"* (John 8:36).

What are we free from? Romans 8:1–2 explains, *"Therefore, there is now no condemnation for those who are in Christ Jesus, because through Christ Jesus the law of the Spirit who gives life has set you free from the law of sin and death."* Paul continues, *"You have been set free from sin and have become slaves to righteousness"* (Romans 6:18).

Once you know Jesus, it's important to remember that Jesus sent a Helper to guide us in truth. 2 Corinthians 3:17 says, *"Now the Lord is the Spirit, and where the Spirit of the Lord is, there is freedom."* Following the prompts of the Holy Spirit will always lead you in the direction of truth.

The half-brother of Jesus chimes in with some insight on this: *"But whoever looks intently into the perfect law that gives freedom, and continues in it—not forgetting what they have heard, but doing it—they will be blessed in what they do"* (James 1:25). God will bless our lives if we do what is true.

Charles Ryrie wrote, "Obedience to God's command brings freedom; disobedience brings bondage."[159] William MacDonald comments on John 8:31–32, saying,

> This means they continue in the teachings of Christ. They do not turn aside from Him. True faith always has the quality of permanence. They were not saved by abiding in His Word, but they abide in His Word because they are saved. Those who truly know the Lord Jesus are delivered from sin, they walk in the light, and are led by the Holy Spirit of God.[160]

Let's continue on to the topic of worshipping the Lord. Jesus makes a very telling comment in John 4:23, saying, *"Yet a time is coming and has now come when the true worshipers will worship the Father in the Spirit and in truth, for they are the kind of worshipers the Father seeks."* Here, the word true is again used in the context of our walk with Jesus. I want to be in the group Jesus mentioned in that verse.

John MacArthur describes this true worship:

> Jesus' point that in light of his coming as Messiah and Saviour, worshipers will be identified, not by a particular shrine or location, but by their worship of the Father through the Son. True worshipers are all those everywhere who worshiped God through the Son, from the heart.[161]

As you can see, embodying the truth is a major foundation of our walk with Jesus. Truth is one of those words that can be read in a second but take a lifetime to achieve—and we only achieve it with the help of the Holy Spirit.

Application. Here are three ways to apply this truth to your life today:

1. With God's help and the Spirit's direction, tell the truth, the whole truth, and nothing but the truth.
2. Never say "Honest to God…" Let your "Yes" be "Yes" and your "No" be "No."
3. Be a true worshiper in praise, prayer, study, and doing what is right.

The next phrase in Philippians 4:8 says *"whatever is noble."*

Observation. The New International Version uses the word "noble," but most other translations, such as the King James Version, use the word "honest," while the New American Standard, New Living Translation, and English Standard Version use the word "honourable." It comes from the Greek adjective *semnos*, meaning honest or honourable.

Collins English Dictionary describes noble this way: "of or characterized by high moral qualities."[162]

John MacArthur describes it in these terms: "The Greek term means 'worthy of respect.' Believers are to meditate on whatever is worthy of awe and adoration, i.e., the sacred as opposed to the profane."[163] By honourable, Chuck Swindoll explains, "Paul means we are to think on what is revered, not what is cheap or superficial. He is not talking about slap-happy, simplistic thinking. We are to dwell on deep truth."[164]

Charles Ryrie simply states, "noble = worthy of respect."[165] Respect is not a widely implemented practice these days. There is very little respect for anything, let alone those in authority over us. This should be a strong trait of a believer in Jesus Christ, as we are told in Scripture to be respectful of others, especially those in authority, and to do what is right.

One of my favourite verses regarding wives and mothers is found in Proverbs 31:10, which tells us, *"A wife of noble character who can find? She is worth far more than rubies."* It isn't impossible, but it's very hard to find a wife like this one. A noble, honest, and honourable wife is truly a gift from God, and I am thankful that through the Lord's grace, and certainly through nothing I've done to deserve it, He brought me such a wife. I could spend many pages discussing the virtues and qualities of the love of my life. After forty-three years of marriage, I still get excited when she walks into a room! But I need to stay on track…

These are some of the traits of a noble and honourable woman, wife, and mother:

- She is worth more than rubies.
- People are highly confident in her.
- She brings good all the days of her life, not harm.
- She works with eager hands.
- She provides for her family.
- She considers a field and buys it; out of her earnings, she plants a vineyard.
- She sets about her work vigorously. Her arms are strong for the task.
- She sees that her trading is profitable, and her lamp does not go out at night.
- She opens her arms to the poor and extends her hands to the needy.
- She speaks wisdom, and faithful instruction is on her tongue.
- She watches over the affairs of her household and does not eat the bread of idleness.
- Her children rise up and call her blessed, her husband also, and he praises her.

I realize this list can appear dated to modern readers, and it can also be used to describe a noble man or father, but the context is very relevant for today. The point is that in this world of disrespect, we as Christians are to think oppositely to the thinking of the world.

Just imagine a family that embodies the traits of the noble woman described above. Wouldn't it be great to be defined like the woman in Proverbs 31:29? That verse says, *"Many women do noble things, but you surpass them all."* That's the goal we should shoot for. That's the *Rocky III* way of thinking—go for it!

Application. There are three ways you can apply this verse today:

1. With God's help, live a noble, honest, and honourable life.
2. Be respectful to others, especially those in authority.

3. Set a goal to do noble things, with a target to surpass them all!

The next phrase from Philippians 4:8 tells us to think on *"whatever is right."*

Observation. William Penn, who founded the U.S. state of Pennsylvania, said, "Right is right, even if everyone is against it, and wrong is wrong, even if everyone is for it."[166] In all honesty, that should tell us all we need to know about this verse; I truly believe most people do know the difference between right and wrong.

In the world today, people feel that they can determine right and wrong according to their own standards. There are undoubtedly grey areas in life, but according to the world, everything is grey. Not so with God. Ultimately, it's not so important to understand right and wrong; what's important is doing right and not doing wrong.

Again, I truly believe that people know, deep down, right from wrong. However, we don't like to be told what we can't do. But as Christians, we are to do the right things.

Directly after Paul wrote the great salvation verses of Ephesians 2:8–9—which says, *"For it is by grace you have been saved, through faith—and this is not from yourselves, it is the gift of God—not by works, so that no one can boast"*—he followed them up with this incredible instruction: *"For we are God's handiwork, created in Christ Jesus to do good works, which God prepared in advance for us to do"* (Ephesians 2:10).

God created us to do what is right and good. That is the DNA of the Christian faith.

James takes this to the next level in James 4:17: *"If anyone, then, knows the good they ought to do and doesn't do it, it is sin for them."*

We are built to do the right things—that's how we were created by God, to live according to His standards, not the standards the world establishes. Please indulge me as I say this again: this is not a works-based righteousness to earn your way to heaven; that can only happen by receiving the gift of God through Jesus Christ our Lord and Saviour.

Chuck Swindoll adds in his commentary of this verse:

things that are upright and just and fair. The apostle does not see himself as above this rule. It is a Godly standard that calls us all to account and to a higher virtue. It urges us to imitate our all-good heavenly Father. We are to think on those things that stand in stark contrast to evil and wrong.[167]

John MacArthur uses the word "just" and defines it this way: "The believer is to think in harmony with God's divine standard of holiness."[168] Our standard in life should be holiness, and that's what we should continually work to attain in our lives.

Warren Wiersbe puts it this way:

> This means "worthy of respect and right." There are many things that are not respectable, and Christians should not think about these things. This does not mean we hide our heads in the sand and avoid what is unpleasant and displeasing, but it does mean we do not focus our attention on dishonourable things and permit them to control our thoughts.[169]

So, as you can see, we are called to do whatever is right.

When approaching one of those rare grey areas, turn to the Scriptures to find the answer. Make it a matter of prayer and truly wait for the prompting of the Holy Spirit. When you do a wrong thing, a trail of deceit begins that requires an enormous amount of energy to later keep straight. Once you start down the road of deceit, it only builds. Before long, you find yourself in a world that is stressful and harmful to you and those around you. When you do what is right, you can move on to the next things in life with no regrets.

Application. This verse can be applied in three ways:

1. Live a life where right is right, even if everyone is against you.
2. Stand up for the things that are right, just, and fair.
3. When grey areas appear, lean on Scripture and prayer.

Philippians 4:8 then tell us to think on *"whatever is pure."*

Observation. Purity isn't a word often used today, but it's a beautiful character trait of a believer in Jesus Christ. Chuck Swindoll states,

> Next, Paul indicates that which is pure. This cuts right to the intentions of the heart. Our thoughts should stem from pure motives that can withstand God's scrutiny. They should be chaste and undefiled, not smutty, shabby or soiled.[170]

Many scriptures use the word pure, and they are very powerful. We need to pay attention to this small word. As I reviewed it, I found that the best definition is found in the biblical use of specific verses. Let's begin in the Old Testament.

> *And the words of the Lord are flawless, like silver purified in a crucible, like gold refined seven times.*
> —Psalm 12:6

> *The fear of the Lord is pure, enduring forever.*
> —Psalm 19:9

> *The one who has clean hands and a pure heart, who does not trust in an idol or swear by a false god. They will receive blessing from the Lord and vindication from God their Savior.*
> —Psalm 24:4–5

This next verse was written by David after his transgression with Bathsheba and he felt distant from the Lord. Although he was king at the time, he couldn't function without the Lord in his life. You can almost feel the desperation in his voice as he pleads with God:

> *Create in me a pure heart, O God, and renew a steadfast spirit within me. Do not cast me from your presence or take your Holy Spirit from me. Restore to me the joy of your salvation and grant me a willing spirit, to sustain me.*
> —Psalm 51:10–12

> The Lord detests the thoughts of the wicked, but gracious words are pure in his sight.
>
> —Proverbs 15:26

As we move to the New Testament, Scripture continues to emphasize the importance of the word pure. In the Sermon on the Mount, Jesus explains in the Beatitudes what a pure heart means to Him and the promise that follows. This is an incredible verse: *"Blessed are the pure in heart, for they will see God"* (Matthew 5:8). Now that's a promise you want to have in your life!

Paul sets a goal in 1 Timothy 1:5: *"The goal of this command is love, which comes from a pure heart and a good conscience and a sincere faith."* We hold responsibility for our purity. Then 1 Timothy 5:22 tells us not to *"share in the sins of others. Keep yourself pure."*

Continuing on in terms of actions we must take, 2 Timothy 2:22 tells us, *"Flee the evil desires of youth and pursue righteousness, faith, love and peace, along with those who call on the Lord out of a pure heart."* Titus 1:15 says, *"To the pure, all things are pure, but to those who are corrupted and do not believe, nothing is pure."*

James includes a great verse regarding our faith and walk with the Lord. The verse requires us as Christians to have pure motives in our actions: *"Religion that God our Father accepts as pure and faultless is this: to look after orphans and widows in their distress and to keep oneself from being polluted by the world"* (James 1:27).

Later in his epistle, James makes another great statement: *"But the wisdom that comes from heaven is first of all pure; then peace-loving, considerate, submissive, full of mercy and good fruit, impartial and sincere"* (James 3:17). Now that verse contains some serious adjectives!

As I've mentioned before, a single verse in God's Word can change your life. If a person could live out what it says in James 3:17, it would have a massive impact on their life. My hope is that you will find your own great life-changing verses as you continue to mine for gold in the Bible.

We desperately need to embody the word pure in our society today. Young Christian couples in dating relationships are looked upon as aliens in this world for wanting to abstain until they're married. As I've mentioned, the thinking of a Christian is opposite to those in the world.

When you pray to have only pure thoughts, God will honour those prayers. Proverbs 23:7 tells us, *"For as he thinketh in his heart, so is he"* (KJV). Understand that it's essential to have a pure thought life as you grow in your walk with the Lord, and this can only happen through prayer, study, and listening to the Holy Spirit.

William MacDonald wrote,

> In verse 7, Paul has assured the saints that God would garrison their hearts and thoughts in Christ Jesus. But he is not neglectful to remind them that they too have a responsibility in the matter. God does not garrison the thought-life of a person who does not want to be kept pure.[171]

The word pure also refers to the state of our heart. Always remember that God knows your heart; nothing is hidden. Psalm 139:23–24 says, *"Search me, God, and know my heart; test me and know my anxious thoughts. See if there is any offensive way in me, and lead me in the way everlasting."*

Application. Here are three ways you can apply this verse in your life:

1. Set your mind on pure thoughts and run from evil thoughts.
2. Keep away from any form of impurity or evil. That is your responsibility.
3. When helping others, make sure your motives are pure.

Next, Philippians 4:8 uses the phrase *"whatever is lovely."*

Observation. Different forms of the word love are mentioned hundreds of times in the Bible. A concordance is a great reference book to own. Some, like the *Strong's Exhaustive Concordance of the Bible*, list every word in the Bible in alphabetical order by book. Most study Bibles also have a concordance in the back of the book.

If you look up the word love, you'll discover enough Bible verses to study for the rest of your life. As a Christian, love is the basis for everything we believe. The Bible continuously tells us to love one another.

As we've discussed, John was known as the apostle Jesus loved. In his first letter, he wrote a great passage on the glories of love. Please take the time to read what he has to say:

> *Dear friends, since God so loved us, we also ought to love one another. No one has ever seen God; but if we love one another, God lives in us and his love is made complete in us.*
>
> *This is how we know that we live in him and he in us: He has given us of his Spirit. And we have seen and testify that the Father has sent his Son to be the Savior of the world. If anyone acknowledges that Jesus is the Son of God, God lives in them and they in God. And so we know and rely on the love God has for us.*
>
> *God is love. Whoever lives in love lives in God, and God in them. This is how love is made complete among us so that we will have confidence on the day of judgment: In this world we are like Jesus. There is no fear in love. But perfect love drives out fear, because fear has to do with punishment. The one who fears is not made perfect in love.*
>
> *We love because he first loved us. Whoever claims to love God yet hates a brother or sister is a liar. For whoever does not love their brother and sister, whom they have seen, cannot love God, whom they have not seen. And he has given us this command: Anyone who loves God must also love their brother and sister.*
>
> —1 John 4:11–21

What a great portion of Scripture! I've said it before and it's worth repeating: if you could live just this passage, your life would change dramatically. From this verse, you could unpack so many great ideas to bring joy and comfort to your life.

Let's look at a few:

- Love one another.
- If we love one another, God lives in us.
- His love is made complete in us.
- He has given us His Spirit.

- His Son is Saviour of the world.
- God is love.
- We will have confidence on the day of judgement.
- There is no fear in love.
- We love because He first loved us.
- If anyone says "I love God" yet hates his brother, he is a liar.

As great as this scripture is to hear, it must also be lived. Chuck Swindoll makes a very important point regarding the way we come across as Christians:

> We are called to think on whatever is lovely. This refers to things that are amiable, pleasing, and agreeable. How we need that! The evangelical, conservative camp is sometimes seen as the ugly duckling of Protestantism. We get pigeonholed as fighters, the people who have too little tolerance. We get a bad reputation in the eyes of the world when we stand aloof: Unless you walk with us exactly in step, we don't give you the time of day. We think a conversation with an unbeliever is worthless if they don't convert or at least visit a church.[172] How often do we think of what is pleasing, winsome and appealing to everyone?[173]

This comment from Swindoll made me take a moment to stop and think about my approach to others and what happened when I met Jesus. If I'm honest with myself, I've been that person Chuck described. It's important to remember that we don't save anyone; that part is all up to God.

As I go back to the time when I came to Christ, it wasn't because someone browbeat me and attacked my sin. If they had, I would have just fought back, which I had no problem doing when I was a lot younger and unintimidated by most things. No, that approach would have never worked with me. In fact, of all the testimonies of salvation I've heard over the years, never have I heard anyone say they made their decision to follow Jesus through intimidation.

Giving God all the glory, the vessel He used was my mother. My mom is the person I know who came closest to truly demonstrating the unconditional love of Jesus to me. That love, and her letters telling me how much Jesus loved me, was the instrument God used to bring me to faith in Jesus.

We owe God everything for His love for us—everything. There is nothing we could ever do to repay that debt.

The fourth stanza of the hymn "When I Survey the Wondrous Cross" sums this up perfectly:

> Were the whole realm of nature mine,
> that were a present far too small.
> Love so amazing, so divine,
> demands my soul, my life, my all.[174]

How can we not love and forgive our brothers and sisters, whom we can see, and say that we love God, who we cannot see? If we are forgiven, how can we not forgive others?

Throughout my life, things have been done to me that made me want to greatly dislike people and desire revenge. Then I would remember what I myself have been forgiven of, and I can tell you this: no one has wronged me as much as I have wronged our Lord. So how can I not forgive others?

Love conquers all. It covers a multitude of sins. It loves when no one else will love.

I want to conclude this section with some verses that are often read at weddings, although the topic covers more than just marriage:

> *Love is patient, love is kind. It does not envy, it does not boast, it is not proud. It does not dishonor others, it is not self-seeking, it is not easily angered, it keeps no record of wrongs. Love does not delight in evil but rejoices with the truth. It always protects, always trusts, always hopes, always perseveres. Love never fails.*
> —1 Corinthians 13:4–8

A quick test is to remove the word love and insert your name in place of it throughout that passage and see how you stack up. This could be an inventory check to make at the end of each day.

The last verse in the chapter sums up the importance of love. 1 Corinthians 13:13 says, *"And now these three remain: faith, hope and love. But the greatest of these is love."*

Application. We can apply this passage in three ways:

1. Love and forgive others in the same way Jesus has done.
2. Share a faith of love and mercy to others. Be patient.
3. Resolve any issues you have with others and show them love.

We then read, in Philippians 4:8, the phrase *"whatever is admirable."* **Observation.** Chuck Swindoll explains it this way:

Finally, we are to fix our minds on what is admirable—that which is praiseworthy, attractive, and of good report. Think of this category as containing the things that are fit for God to hear. For example, once during a forty-minute drive, I decided to think about three particular individuals. As I dwelt on the reasons they meant so much to me, the "admirable," I was remarkably refreshed in my inner person. This exercise led to true contentment; the kind Paul speaks of in Philippians 4:11.[175]

Have you ever admired someone? What are the traits they show that make you want to look up to them?

As I was reading Swindoll's words, my mind shifted to the people I have admired over the years—and one person specifically came to mind: the person who spent many hours teaching and mentoring me. When I look back to when I met this man more than forty years ago, I am amazed at the ways in which he still impacts my life. I will always thank God for bringing him into my life at a time when I was insecure in my career. As my career grew, we continued to stay in touch and he always seemed to take time to teach and encourage me.

May more people be "admirable" in this way to others, and may God give me the care and concern for others to do for them what my friend did for me.

While I was writing this, my mentor emailed me a photograph of the two of us from the mid-80s. I immediately phoned him and told him that I had been in the process of writing about him when his email arrived. The timing was just another small blessing from God, an opportunity to take a break and spend time with someone who changed my life.

The King James Version and New American Standard Bible use the phrase "of good report." These are wonderful words to live by—admirable and of good report—and should be qualities we strive for in our lives.

When you live this way, you can make a difference not only to others but to yourself. It's a life of honesty and integrity, not covering things up or doing things in an underhanded way.

When people think of you, do these terms come to mind? The English Standard Version uses the word "commendable," which John MacArthur defines as "that which is highly regarded or thought well of. It refers to what is generally considered reputable in this world, such as kindness, courtesy and respect for others."[176] By nature, we aren't built this way. We need to lean on the help of the Holy Spirit to direct our ways.

A good benchmark to becoming admirable is found in Proverbs 3:5–6, which says, *"Trust in the Lord with all your heart and lean not on your own understanding; in all your ways submit to him, and he will make your paths straight."* The KJV uses the expression *"he shall direct thy paths."* We need the direction that comes from God found in His Word.

When you decide to admire someone, make sure they're worthy of that honour due to a good report and their walk with Jesus.

Application. This passage can be applied to your life in three ways:

1. Live a life that is admirable and of good report, honouring our Lord and Saviour Jesus Christ.
2. Trust in the Lord with all your heart. He will direct your paths.
3. Be a person who mentors others using scriptural principles.

Finally, Philippians 4:8 ends this way: *"if anything is excellent or praiseworthy—think about such things."*

Rocky III and the Bible

Observation. In 1982, author Tom Peters wrote a book called *In Search of Excellence*,[177] and he followed it up in 1985 with *Passion for Excellence*.[178] I was extremely fortunate enough to see him speak about this topic in person. On that day, I was joined by my mentor and his wife, and we got there early in order to claim a seat in the front row.

Needless to say, it was a great presentation! Peters never read from notes or a script, and his only visual aid was slides. Remember, this was in the 80s! He had a slide projector, and as he advanced to each new slide, a picture of a company or person would appear; he would then tell the story of how excellence had shone forth in that particular example.

My mentor had a copy of one of Peters's books with him, and just as the presentation ended he told me it would be great to see if he could get the author to sign it. The place was packed with thousands of people, so as soon as Peters sat down at the conclusion of the presentation, I snatched the book from my mentor's hand, quickly walked up to the front, and asked him to sign the book for my mentor who had done so much for me.

"Sure!" Tom replied. "What's his name?"

I later found out that a photographer had been taking photos during the presentation, and several of the pictures taken showed my mentor and Tom Peters together. I contacted the person who ran the conference and asked if there was any way I could get copies of the photos. It took months, but he finally sent me copies of some great shots of my mentor with Tom Peters, which I had framed and sent to him. He told me that was excellent!

What a great title for a book that is: *In Search of Excellence*. That's how you should view the study of God's Word. Look intently and you will find things that are excellent in living your life for the Lord.

Studying the Bible is truly comparable to mining for hidden treasure, except it's not as hard to find when you begin your journey through God's Word. Although I use mining as an example, I have to admit that I've never worked in a mine. However, I have been in a uranium mine in northern Saskatchewan, on Cigar Lake. The process was to delve deep into the earth with drills the size of a large vehicle. We were, I believe, a hundred stories below the earth's surface, and the workers had to freeze the walls prior to drilling or else water would flood the mine.

Whatever they pay those guys, it's not enough. They would mine for long periods of time before finding what they were looking for, eventually striking gold—or in this case, uranium.

The difference in mining for treasure in God's Word is that there is gold on every page.

Collins English Dictionary defines excellent as, "exceptionally good; extremely meritorious, superior."[179] I must confess that I had to use the assistance of a thesaurus to better understand the word "meritorious." It was worth looking up, as several words are associated with it: commendable, praiseworthy, worthy, and admirable. The word "excellent" could also be easily applied to God's Word.

When you focus on the things that are excellent listed above, it will not only change your mind, but your attitude as well. This is what the passage from Philippians 4 wants us to think about and strive toward.

Chuck Swindoll adds, "As believers, our minds have been freed to think on these things rather than on the many negatives and selfish thoughts that could consume us every day."[180] MacDonald concludes his commentary on this verse, "Virtue, of course, speaks of moral excellence; and praiseworthy, something that deserves to be commended."[181]

Let's move on now to the final word used in this incredible list compiled by Paul: praiseworthy. It's time to take inventory of the things a person might feel are worthy of praise.

It's a good exercise to list the things that you feel are praiseworthy. Warren Wiersbe comments,

> If it has virtue, it will motivate us to do better, and if it has praise, it is worth commending others. No Christian can afford to waste "mind-power" on thoughts that tear down or that would tear others down if these thoughts were shared.[182]

Make sure you're praising things that are truly praiseworthy in the eyes of our Lord and Saviour Jesus Christ, who deserves all our praise.

Application. At last, here are three ways to apply these truths in your life:

1. Mine for the treasures in God's Word and live them.
2. Have a mindset of one who searches for areas of excellence in your life, honouring Jesus Christ.
3. Because God is praiseworthy, give Him your constant worship and praise.

In summary, the eight words in Philippians 4:8—true, noble, right, pure, lovely, admirable, excellent, and praiseworthy—are certainly worth the time to study and apply to your daily life. Warren Wiersbe wraps up this verse in a neat package:

> If you compare this list to David's description of the Word of God in Psalm 19:7–9, you will see a parallel. The Christian who fills his heart and mind with God's Word will have a "built-in radar" for detecting wrong thoughts. Right thinking is the result of daily meditation on the Word of God.[183]

Psalm 19:7–9 says,

> *The law of the Lord is perfect, refreshing the soul. The statutes of the Lord are trustworthy, making wise the simple. The precepts of the Lord are right, giving joy to the heart. The commands of the Lord are radiant, giving light to the eyes. The fear of the Lord is pure, enduring forever. The decrees of the Lord are firm, and all of them are righteous.*

May God truly use these words to encourage you to meditate and study His Word.

Philippians 4:9 tells us, "*Whatever you have learned or received or heard from me, or seen in me—put it into practice. And the God of peace will be with you.*"

Observation. Let's start by discussing the second half of that verse. When you live a life as described in this passage, it ends with a great promise: "*And the God of peace will be with you.*" This is one more in a long list of comforting words that are strewn throughout God's Word. It is true peace to know that the Creator of the universe is not only with you, but He brings you along with Him on this journey.

The peace spoken of here is not the normal, everyday peace offered by the world. As Jesus said, as He was about to leave the disciples, *"Peace I leave with you; my peace I give you. I do not give to you as the world gives. Do not let your hearts be troubled and do not be afraid"* (John 14:27). The peace of the Lord Jesus is much greater than anything the world could ever hope to give.

When Jesus was born in Bethlehem, it was described this way: *"Suddenly a great company of the heavenly host appeared with the angel, praising God and saying, 'Glory to God in the highest heaven, and on earth peace to those on whom his favor rests'"* (Luke 2:13–14).

The word peace was spoken almost immediately by the angels after the birth of Christ. Jesus came to save souls, offering a peace like none other, since it came from above.

As Paul brings the letter to the Romans to a close, he writes in Romans 15:33, *"The God of peace be with you all. Amen."*

Jesus continued to teach His disciples, mentioning peace again in John 16:33: *"I have told you these things, so that in me you may have peace. In this world you will have trouble. But take heart! I have overcome the world."*

Earlier in Philippians 4, Paul wrote, and this is worth repeating: *"And the peace of God, which transcends all understanding, will guard your hearts and your minds in Christ Jesus."* And in the Old Testament, the Lord made a promise in Psalm 85:8, *"I will listen to what God the Lord says; he promises peace to his people, his faithful servants."* God is the source of true peace and gives us perfect peace in times of trouble.

William MacDonald says,

> Those who are faithful in following the example of the apostle are promised the God of peace will be with them. In verse 7, the peace of God is the portion of those who are prayerful; here the God of peace is the companion of those who are holy. The thought here is that God will make Himself very near and dear in the present experiences of all whose lives are embodiments of the truth.[184]

Warren Wiersbe has a great take on this portion of Scripture:

> The peace of God is one test of whether or not we are in the will of God. "Let the peace that Christ can give keep on acting as umpire in your hearts" (Col 3:15 WMS). If we are walking with the Lord, then the peace of God and God of peace exercise influence over our hearts. Whenever we disobey, we lose that peace and we know we have done something wrong. God's peace is the umpire that calls us "out!"[185]

Application. Here are three ways to apply this verse:

1. Be thankful for the kind of peace you have in your life that can only come from Jesus.
2. When your peace fails, examine your life and get back in step with God.
3. Live a life, and be a person, of peace.

Now back to the first half of Philippians 4:9, which says, *"Whatever you have learned or received or heard from me, or seen in me—put it into practice."*

Observation. As we conclude this chapter, Warren Wiersbe advises that when we disobey, we lose our peace.[186] This is a great transition into the final section, where the rubber finally meets the road.

As you read through this book, I hope you came to see that following Jesus is very exciting, as long as you truly follow Him. You can't have it both ways. Jesus will never leave you or forsake you once you are His child, but the journey can be tough when you leave His service and walk down your own road.

What I'm about to state, and it's something I have stated several times throughout our journey, is that you cannot earn your way into heaven; there aren't enough good deeds you could perform to reach that goal. This is what separates Christianity from all other religions. As Romans tells us, *"There is no one righteous, not even one"* (Romans 3:10).

It is only by the saving grace of Jesus taking away the sins of the world, and dying on the cross for you and me, that we are saved from eternal damnation. Only when you repent of your sins and receive Jesus as your Lord and Saviour will you be saved.

I reaffirm this only because the rest of the chapter will be written to Christians and the work we are to do after we receive Jesus, not because we have to but because we want to out of our thankfulness for the greatest gift of all: God's Son Jesus, given as a sacrifice for our sins.

Now that we are sharing the correct perspective, let's talk about what it means to put this into practice. In James 1:22, the half-brother of Jesus made a statement that needs no explanation: *"Do not merely listen to the word, and so deceive yourselves. Do what it says."* That, my friends, is what we need to do, in a nutshell. It's great advice for living the Christian life.

This is easy to say, but take heart: it is a lifelong journey. As stated earlier, sin will always be around and Satan will continue to attack, but that doesn't mean we give up. We have Philippians 1:6 to hold on to: *"being confident of this, that he who began a good work in you will carry it on to completion until the day of Christ Jesus."*

Charles Ryrie puts it this way: "God will continue His good work of grace in them until the consummation and the day of Christ Jesus (the day when Christ returns)."[187]

William MacDonald states, "As the apostle thinks of the good start the believers have made in the Christian life, he is confident that God will finish the good works He has begun."[188]

We are not alone in this journey with Jesus, and He has left us the Holy Spirit to lead and guide us. Our peace will come when we listen and act upon that leading. When you try to have it both ways, you end up like the people in Galatians 3:3: *"Are you so foolish? After beginning by means of the Spirit, are you now trying to finish by means of the flesh?"*

Charles Ryrie says of this verse,

> Paul brought the gospel to them and the Spirit worked in them. Yet now they were reverting to flesh works in the hope that a combination of faith (Spirit) and works (flesh) would work more easily and better.[189]

The word "beginning" in Galatians 2:2 is the same word used in Philippians 1:6 for "began," and both times it's used in reference to salvation itself.

John MacArthur states, "When God begins a work of salvation in a person, He finishes and perfects that work; the verb 'bring it to completion' points to the eternal security of the Christian."[190] This won't happen overnight, and we will experience times of backsliding and discouragement. But take heart: He who began this work will complete it!

I know, I know, I've said this before, but one of my all-time favourite scriptures, which encapsulates why I study the Bible, comes from 2 Timothy 2:15: *"Do your best to present yourself to God as one approved, a worker who does not need to be ashamed and who correctly handles the word of truth."*

As with any trade, you need to have the tools and know-how to be effective and hone your skills. The more you use the tools, the better the craftsperson you become.

This is what Paul was trying to teach his apprentice, Timothy.

Romans 1:16 states, *"For I am not ashamed of the gospel, because it is the power of God that brings salvation to everyone who believes: first to the Jew, then to the Gentile."* I don't want to be ashamed of the gospel, and one way to make sure we aren't ashamed is to clearly understand what it means.

My hope is to continue to increase this skill by studying the Word of God and correctly and truthfully sharing my faith with others.

Charles Ryrie says, "[C]orrectly handles. I.e., in both analysis and presentation—in contrast to the inane interpretation of false teachers."[191] Don't take at face value what others say without the intense scrutiny of God's Word. I appreciate the opinions of others, but when they're contrary to the Bible, we need to stay away from their teachings.

The way to truly understand when someone is leading you astray is to confirm their teaching of the Bible. This is paramount to living a full Christian life. Considering the price that was paid for you and me, we need to step up to the plate and be certain of the teaching we're listening to.

John MacArthur makes an incredible point regarding this passage:

> "Do your best." This word denotes zealous persistence in accomplishing a goal. Timothy, like all who preach and teach the

word, was to give his maximum effort to impart God's word completely, accurately, and clearly to his hearers. This is crucial to counter the disastrous effects of false teaching...

..."rightly handling" literally "cutting it straight"—a reference to the exactness demanded by such trades as carpentry, masonry, and Paul's trade of leather working and tentmaking. Precision and accuracy are required in biblical interpretation, beyond all other enterprises, because the interpreter is handling God's word. Anything less is shameful.[192]

He then concludes his commentary on 2 Timothy 2:15: "All Scripture in general and the gospel message in particular."[193] Study and apply the Word of God to your life and just watch what happens.

There is another passage that well explains the power of the Word of God. Read and listen as Paul describes this power in Hebrews 4:12–13:

> *For the word of God is alive and active. Sharper than any double-edged sword, it penetrates even to dividing soul and spirit, joints and marrow; it judges the thoughts and attitudes of the heart. Nothing in all creation is hidden from God's sight. Everything is uncovered and laid bare before the eyes of him to whom we must give account.*

We cannot hide from God forever. There will come times of mourning, of reckoning, and this is when we need to praise Jesus for taking away the sin of the world.

As you study the Bible, be prepared to face the shortcomings in your life. You will see the holiness of God and see yourself for who you are. This is not a bad thing, because not only does it show the power to save but it gives you the instruction to transform yourself into the person God wants you to be.

Charles Ryrie points out,

> Here meaning His inspired Word, the Scriptures. living and active. It has the power to reach to the inmost parts of one's

personality and to judge the innermost thoughts—soul and spirit. This means that the Word pierces to the depths of soul and spirit, not between the two.[194]

There is some serious power in the pages of this amazing book.

As I bring this chapter to a close, I want to return to the idea that I found *Rocky III* to be one of the most motivating stories ever told. To watch the first three Rocky movies, to see where he came from as a character and how he made it to the top, is an inspirational experience, to say the least.

The verses covered in this chapter had the same motivational effect on me. If you ever need a pick-me-up, read Philippians 4:4–9. The words, theme, and phrases are extremely uplifting and relevant for today. Rocky came back from defeat, and in the end he defeated Clubber to become the champion once again. What a great ending to the movie!

Let's wrap up with a charge Paul gave to Timothy. This could be one of the best motivational speeches ever put to paper! Although written thousands of years ago, it's truly needed today.

> *In the presence of God and of Christ Jesus, who will judge the living and the dead, and in view of his appearing and his kingdom, I give you this charge: Preach the word; be prepared in season and out of season; correct, rebuke and encourage—with great patience and careful instruction. For the time will come when people will not put up with sound doctrine. Instead, to suit their own desires, they will gather around them a great number of teachers to say what their itching ears want to hear. They will turn their ears away from the truth and turn aside to myths. But you, keep your head in all situations, endure hardship, do the work of an evangelist, discharge all the duties of your ministry.*
> —2 Timothy 4:1–5 (emphasis added)

Remember that the "But you" mentioned at the end of this passage is actually *you!*

We are in a society where anything goes, and Jesus has been thrown to the curb. The important thing to remember is that we shouldn't conform to this world and its teaching, but instead make Jesus the Lord of our lives and live with the Bible as our policy and procedures manual—with the leading of the Holy Spirit, of course.

Take this passage to heart and be a leader and champion for Jesus. May your journey through God's Word take you to new heights and new places you never dreamed of going. As you head on your own journey, give everything to our Lord and Saviour Jesus Christ.

Conclusion

Well, we've come to the end of the journey through God's Word and I hope you have found it helpful, and even life-changing. To the unbeliever, my hope and prayer is that this book will have opened your heart and mind to finally meet Jesus Christ and receive Him as your personal Lord and Saviour.

Before we finish, you must settle this issue, and you can do it right now. You can live with full assurance of your salvation by surrendering your life to Jesus, repenting of your sins, and believing in His sacrifice on your behalf. He paid it all! Don't live another day without Jesus.

After you've received this free gift of salvation, it's critical to find a church that preaches from the Bible as its foundation; you need to be fed spiritually on a regular basis.

And finally, to make your walk with the Lord complete, you need to study your Bible and learn how to apply it and live out its teachings. I guarantee that it will change your life. Hopefully, you will come to see from this book that God can truly answer every question and handle any concern that may come along in your life.

To the believer, my prayer is that you will see that simply going to church isn't enough. Fortunately, I attend a church where the Bible is preached every Sunday and I am very well fed, spiritually speaking. But in the society we find ourselves in today, we need more. It's a necessity to spend time every day in God's Word, not only reading but also digging deep in study.

Finally, and most importantly, as Christians we must apply what we've learned to our daily lives.

It's only fitting to conclude this book with some incredible verses to help carry you through almost any circumstance in life. We'll finish strong with a great promise from God's Word:

> *But we have this treasure in jars of clay to show that this all-surpassing power is from God and not from us. We are hard pressed on every side, but not crushed; perplexed, but not in despair; persecuted, but not abandoned; struck down, but not destroyed…*
>
> *Therefore we do not lose heart. Though outwardly we are wasting away, yet inwardly we are being renewed day by day. For our light and momentary troubles are achieving for us an eternal glory that far outweighs them all. So we fix our eyes not on what is seen, but on what is unseen, since what is seen is temporary, but what is unseen is eternal.*
>
> —1 Corinthians 4:7–9, 16–18

By studying the Word of God, you are renewing your hearts and minds, preparing yourself to fight a battle you cannot lose.

When I concluded my three years of teaching high school men to prepare them biblically to enter university, their parents had a dinner for me which I will never forget. At that dinner, they presented me with a painting with a quote from Billy Graham: "I've read the last page of the Bible. It's all going to turn out all right." Rejoice in this and realize that there is nothing the world can do to take away our salvation. If you have received Jesus as your Lord and Saviour, you have it for eternity.

Let me close with the great words of Romans 8:31, "*What, then, shall we say in response to these things? If God is for us, who can be against us?*" And then Paul continued with an incredible statement of our security in the Lord:

> *For I am convinced that neither death nor life, neither angels nor demons, neither the present nor the future, nor any powers, neither*

height nor depth, nor anything else in all creation, will be able to separate us from the love of God that is in Christ Jesus our Lord.
—Romans 8:38–39

To God be the glory!

Endnotes

CHAPTER TWO

1. Charles Caldwell Ryrie, *Ryrie Study Bible, Expanded Edition* (Chicago, IL: Moody Press, 1992), 802.
2. Ibid.
3. Ibid., 803.

CHAPTER THREE

4. John MacArthur, *The MacArthur Study Bible* (Wheaton, IL: Crossway, 2010), 1371.
5. Ibid., 1372.
6. William MacDonald, *The Believer's Bible Commentary* (Nashville, TN: Thomas Nelson, 1995), 1230.
7. MacArthur, *The MacArthur Study Bible*, 1372.

CHAPTER FOUR

8. Ibid., 1654.
9. Don Fleming, *The World's Bible Dictionary* (Iowa Falls, IA: World Bible Publishers, 1990), 375.
10. MacDonald, *The Believer's Bible Commentary*, 1704.
11. MacArthur, *The MacArthur Study Bible*, 1660.
12. John MacArthur, *Daily Readings from the Life of Christ* (Chicago, IL: Moody Publishers, 2008), 236.

13 John MacArthur, *Hard to Believe* (Nashville, TN: Thomas Nelson, 2003), 143.
14 Fleming, *The World's Bible Dictionary*, 160.
15 Warren Wiersbe, *The Bible Exposition Commentary, New Testament, Volume 2* (Colorado Springs, CO: Cook Communication, 2003), 19.
16 Ryrie, *Ryrie Study Bible, Expanded Edition*, 1893.
17 *The New Illustrated Bible Dictionary* (Nashville, TN: Thomas Nelson, 1995), 439.
18 Fleming, *The World's Bible Dictionary*, 127.
19 MacDonald, *The Believer's Bible Commentary*, 1918.
20 Ibid.
21 Fleming, *The World's Bible Dictionary*, 53.
22 Ryrie, *Ryrie Study Bible, Expanded Edition*, 1624.
23 MacArthur, *Hard to Believe*, 132–133.
24 MacArthur, *The MacArthur Study Bible*, 1668.
25 MacDonald, *The Believer's Bible Commentary*, 1721.
26 Ryrie, *Ryrie Study Bible, Expanded Edition*, 1741.
27 MacDonald, *The Believer's Bible Commentary*, 1722.
28 Ibid., 1728.
29 Isaac Watts, "When I Survey the Wondrous Cross," 1707.
30 Zig Ziglar, *See You at the Top* (Gretna, LA: Pelican Publishing Company, 2000), 228.
31 Ryrie, *Ryrie Study Bible, Expanded Edition*, 1744.
32 MacArthur, *The MacArthur Study Bible*, 1671.
33 MacDonald, *The Believer's Bible Commentary*, 1728.

CHAPTER FIVE

34 Author unknown. Found at: Rachel Wojo, "For God So Loved... the Greatest List," *Rachel Wojo*. February 12, 2014 (https://rachelwojo.com/god-loved-greatest-list/).
35 W.E. Vine, *Vine's Complete Expository Dictionary* (Nashville, TN: Thomas Nelson, 1996), 271.
36 Ibid., 382.
37 *The New Illustrated Bible Dictionary*, 775.

Endnotes

38 *Collins English Dictionary* (New York, NY: HarperCollins, 2004), 657.
39 Capitalizing the W in "Word" means that this refers to God.
40 Vine, *Vine's Complete Expository Dictionary*, 61.
41 Ibid., 294.
42 Ibid., 467.
43 Ibid., 207.
44 MacArthur, *The MacArthur Study Bible*, 1541.

CHAPTER SIX

45 MacDonald, *The Believer's Bible Commentary*, 564.
46 Ryrie, *Ryrie Study Bible, Expanded Edition*, 812.
47 Can you imagine living under that incredible burden?
48 Warren Wiersbe, *The Bible Exposition Commentary, Wisdom and Poetry* (Colorado Springs, CO: Cook Communication, 2003), 115.
49 MacDonald, *The Believer's Bible Commentary*, 564.
50 Ibid., 565.
51 Wiersbe, *The Bible Exposition Commentary, Wisdom and Poetry*, 116.
52 MacArthur, *The MacArthur Study Bible*, 745.
53 Karen Dockery, Johnnie Godwiun, and Phillis Godwin, *The Student Bible Dictionary* (Nashville, TN: Holman Bible Publishers, 2000), 239.
54 *Collins English Dictionary*, 1814.
55 Ibid.
56 Wiersbe, *The Bible Exposition Commentary, Wisdom and Poetry*, 117.
57 MacDonald, *The Believer's Bible Commentary*, 565.
58 Ryrie, *Ryrie Study Bible, Expanded Edition*, 1467.
59 MacDonald, *The Believer's Bible Commentary*, 565.
60 MacArthur, *The MacArthur Study Bible*, 745.
61 Edward Mote, "My Hope Is Built on Nothing Less," 1834.

CHAPTER SEVEN

62 MacArthur, *The MacArthur Study Bible*, 1764.
63 Martin Luther, "A Mighty Fortress Is Our God," 1529.

64 *Collins English Dictionary*, 1456.
65 MacArthur, *The MacArthur Study Bible*, 1768.
66 MacDonald, *The Believer's Bible Commentary*, 1952.
67 William Penn, "Quotations from William Penn," *USHistory.org*. Date of access: December 17, 2020 (www.ushistory.org/penn/quotes.htm).
68 Dockery, Godwiun, and Godwin, *The Student Bible Dictionary*, 234.
69 Debbie McDaniel, "The Armor of Christian Warfare," *Crosswalk*. September 24, 2002 (https://www.crosswalk.com/faith/spiritual-life/the-armor-of-christian-warfare-1149596.html).
70 Ryrie, *Ryrie Study Bible, Expanded Edition*, 1787.
71 "What Is the Peace of God? Its Biblical Meaning and Practical Benefits," *Christianity.com*. March 8, 2019 (https://www.christianity.com/wiki/god/what-is-the-peace-of-god-biblical-meaning.html).
72 Fleming, *The World's Bible Dictionary*, 127.
73 MacArthur, *The MacArthur Study Bible*, 1769.
74 "The Sword of the Roman Army," *Reliks.com*. Date of access: November 19, 2020 (https://www.reliks.com/functional-swords/types/gladius/).
75 MacArthur, *The MacArthur Study Bible*, 1769.
76 Fleming, *The World's Bible Dictionary*, 348.
77 Debbie McDaniel, "The Armor of Christian Warfare," *Crosswalk*. September 24, 2002 (https://www.crosswalk.com/faith/spiritual-life/the-armor-of-christian-warfare-1149596.html).

CHAPTER EIGHT

78 James was the president of the council as he addressed them in Acts 15:13–29.
79 MacArthur, *The MacArthur Study Bible*, 1875.
80 Eugene Peterson, *The Message* (Colorado Springs, CO: NavPress, 2002), 2201.
81 Chuck Swindoll, *The Swindoll Bible* (Carol Stream, IL: Tyndale House, 2017), 1584.

82 Ibid.
83 MacArthur, *The MacArthur Study Bible*, 1879.
84 Swindoll, *The Swindoll Bible*, 1588.
85 Ryrie, *Ryrie Study Bible, Expanded Edition*, 1904.
86 MacDonald, *The Believer's Bible Commentary*, 2229.
87 MacArthur, *The MacArthur Study Bible*, 1879.
88 MacDonald, *The Believer's Bible Commentary*, 2238.
89 Chuck Swindoll, "You Can Make a Difference," *Insight for Living*. June 14, 2016 (https://insightforliving.ca/read/articles/you-can-make-difference).
90 MacDonald, *The Believer's Bible Commentary*, 2228.
91 Wiersbe, *The Bible Exposition Commentary, New Testament, Volume 2*, 354.
92 Swindoll, *The Swindoll Bible*, 1587.
93 MacArthur, *The MacArthur Study Bible*, 1879.
94 MacDonald, *The Believer's Bible Commentary*, 2228.
95 Wiersbe, *The Bible Exposition Commentary, New Testament, Volume 2*, 354.
96 Ryrie, *Ryrie Study Bible, Expanded Edition*, 1904.
97 MacArthur, *The MacArthur Study Bible*, 1880.
98 MacDonald, *The Believer's Bible Commentary*, 2229.
99 MacArthur, *The MacArthur Study Bible*, 1880.
100 Ryrie, *Ryrie Study Bible, Expanded Edition*, 1904.
101 MacDonald, *The Believer's Bible Commentary*, 2229.
102 My hope is that anyone who reads this commentary will sit up and take note of their beliefs. Eternity is in play here and should be taken extremely seriously!
103 Wiersbe, *The Bible Exposition Commentary, New Testament, Volume 2*, 354.

CHAPTER NINE

104 MacArthur, *The MacArthur Study Bible*, 1778.
105 Ibid., 1876.

106 Swindoll, *The Swindoll Bible*, 1585.
107 Wiersbe, *The Bible Exposition Commentary, New Testament*, Volume 2, 338.
108 MacDonald, *The Believer's Bible Commentary*, 2218.
109 *The New Illustrated Bible Dictionary*, 969.
110 This point was covered in further detail earlier, during the discussion of James 2:14–16, in terms of practicing what you preach.
111 MacDonald, *The Believer's Bible Commentary*, 2218.
112 MacArthur, *The MacArthur Study Bible*, 1876.
113 Wiersbe, *The Bible Exposition Commentary, New Testament*, Volume 2, 338.
114 MacArthur, *The MacArthur Study Bible*, 1876.
115 Wiersbe, *The Bible Exposition Commentary, New Testament*, Volume 2, 339.
116 MacDonald, *The Believer's Bible Commentary*, 2219.
117 Ibid.
118 MacArthur, *The MacArthur Study Bible*, 1876.
119 Wiersbe, *The Bible Exposition Commentary, New Testament*, Volume 2, 340.
120 John MacArthur, "Jesus: Liar, Lunatic, or Lord?" *YouTube*. September 16, 2015 (https://www.youtube.com/watch?v=gAp1hKju5u0&ab_channel=GracetoYou).
121 MacArthur, *The MacArthur Study Bible*, 1876.
122 MacDonald, *The Believer's Bible Commentary*, 2219.
123 Wiersbe, *The Bible Exposition Commentary, New Testament*, Volume 2, 340.
124 Ryrie, *Ryrie Study Bible, Expanded Edition*, 1902.
125 MacArthur, *The MacArthur Study Bible*, 1876.
126 Wiersbe, *The Bible Exposition Commentary, New Testament*, Volume 2, 340.
127 Ibid., 341.
128 MacArthur, *The MacArthur Study Bible*, 1877.
129 MacDonald, *The Believer's Bible Commentary*, 2220.
130 Ibid.

Endnotes

CHAPTER TEN

131 Warren Wiersbe, *The Bible Exposition Commentary, Old Testament Genesis, Deuteronomy* (Colorado Springs, CO: Cook Communication, 2003), 397.
132 Swindoll, *The Swindoll Bible*, 1481.
133 MacArthur, *The MacArthur Study Bible*, 1768, 1791.
134 Ibid., 1768.
135 MacDonald, *The Believer's Bible Commentary*, 1951.
136 Ibid., 1979.

CHAPTER ELEVEN

137 *Rocky III*, directed by Sylvester Stallone (Los Angeles, CA: MGM, 1982).
138 MacDonald, *The Believer's Bible Commentary*, 1781.
139 Ibid.
140 MacArthur, *The MacArthur Study Bible*, 1780.
141 Fleming, *The World's Bible Dictionary*, 21.
142 Swindoll, *The Swindoll Bible*, 1146.
143 MacArthur, *The MacArthur Study Bible*, 1790.
144 MacDonald, *The Believer's Bible Commentary*, 1978.
145 MacArthur, *The MacArthur Study Bible*, 1780.
146 Joseph Medlicott Scriven, "What a Friend We Have in Jesus, 1855.
147 Horatio Gates Spafford, "It Is Well with My Soul," 1873.
148 Wiersbe, *The Bible Exposition Commentary, New Testament, Volume 2*, 95.
149 MacArthur, *The MacArthur Study Bible*, 1780.
150 Amy Watson, "Weekly Time Spent Watching TV in Canada 2016–2020, By Age Group," *Statista.com* (https://www.statista.com/statistics/234311/weekly-time-spent-watching-tv-in-canada-by-age-group/).
151 MacArthur, *The MacArthur Study Bible*, 1780.
152 Swindoll, *The Swindoll Bible*, 1494.

153 MacDonald, *The Believer's Bible Commentary*, 1979.
154 *Collins English Dictionary*, 1857.
155 Ibid., 1748.
156 Ibid.
157 There's that word again! I never thought I would use it twice so close together.
158 Swindoll, *The Swindoll Bible*, 1494.
159 Ryrie, *Ryrie Study Bible, Expanded Edition*, 1992.
160 MacDonald, *The Believer's Bible Commentary*, 1517.
161 MacArthur, *The MacArthur Study Bible*, 1544.
162 *Collins English Dictionary*, 1103.
163 MacArthur, *The MacArthur Study Bible*, 1780.
164 Swindoll, *The Swindoll Bible*, 1494.
165 Ryrie, *Ryrie Study Bible, Expanded Edition*, 1828.
166 William Penn, "Quotations from William Penn," USHistory.org. Date of access: December 17, 2020 (www.ushistory.org/penn/quotes.htm).
167 Swindoll, *The Swindoll Bible*, 1494.
168 MacArthur, *The MacArthur Study Bible*, 1780.
169 Wiersbe, *The Bible Exposition Commentary, New Testament, Volume 2*, 95.
170 Swindoll, *The Swindoll Bible*, 1494.
171 MacDonald, *The Believer's Bible Commentary*, 1979.
172 There's a little more truth in that description than I'm comfortable with.
173 Swindoll, *The Swindoll Bible*, 1494.
174 Isaac Watts, "When I Survey the Wondrous Cross," 1707.
175 Ibid.
176 MacArthur, *The MacArthur Study Bible*, 1780.
177 Tom Peters and Robert Waterman, *In Search of Excellence* (New York, NY: Harper and Row, 1982).
178 Tom Peters and Nancy Austin, *Passion for Excellence* (New York, NY: Grand Central Publishing, 1989).
179 *Collins English Dictionary*, 543.
180 Swindoll, *The Swindoll Bible*, 1494.

Endnotes

181 MacDonald, *The Believer's Bible Commentary*, 1979.
182 Wiersbe, *The Bible Exposition Commentary, New Testament, Volume 2*, 96.
183 Ibid.
184 MacDonald, *The Believer's Bible Commentary*, 1979.
185 Wiersbe, *The Bible Exposition Commentary, New Testament, Volume 2*, 96.
186 Ibid.
187 Ryrie, *Ryrie Study Bible, Expanded Edition*, 1823.
188 MacDonald, *The Believer's Bible Commentary*, 1960.
189 Ryrie, *Ryrie Study Bible, Expanded Edition*, 1804.
190 MacArthur, *The MacArthur Study Bible*, 1773.
191 Ryrie, *Ryrie Study Bible, Expanded Edition*, 1863.
192 MacArthur, *The MacArthur Study Bible*, 1829.
193 Ibid.
194 Ryrie, *Ryrie Study Bible, Expanded Edition*, 1883.

www.ingramcontent.com/pod-product-compliance
Lightning Source LLC
Chambersburg PA
CBHW032042150426
43194CB00006B/388